Michigan
Parents' Answer Book

Alice R. McCarthy, Ph.D., President
Patricia B. Peart, Vice President

Bridge Communications, Inc.
306 S. Washington, Suite 208
Royal Oak, MI 48067
(313) 541-0537

Library of Congress Catalog Card Number 88-92392
McCarthy, Alice R.

Michigan Parents' Answer Book

© 1988 by Bridge Communications, Inc.

ISBN 0-9621645-0-X

Printed in the United States of America
10 9 8 7 6 5 4 3 2 1

First Edition - December 1988

Book design by Patricia B. Peart

Michigan PTA

presents the

Parents' Answer Book

by

The Advisory Board
Detroit Free Press Parent Talk Page

Alice R. McCarthy, Ph.D.
Executive Editor

Patricia B. Peart
Editor/Publisher

Marcia M. Danner
Associate Editor

Bridge Communications, Inc.
Royal Oak, Michigan

Distributed by the Michigan PTA

It is a great adventure to be a parent! Nobody promised it would be easy or that you would have all the answers.

The Michigan PTA's service to children, parents and public education spans 70 years. We realize that parenting is not a trained profession and we only seem to learn from experience and advice. So we are proud to sponsor the Michigan Parents' Answer Book.

The role of the Michigan PTA is communication, leadership, training and caring for the well-being of all children.

Together, in partnership – parents, educators, community – we can assure the future of our children.

Carl P. Cohen

President, Michigan PTA

Join your local PTA!

Please contact us for more information

Michigan PTA

1011 North Washington Avenue

Lansing, Michigan 48906

Telephone: (517) 485-4345

Kids: *Who is interested? A myriad of parents, care-giving professionals and diverse groups from government, business and industry, education and religious organizations.*

For those concerned about children, research in disciplines related to the family has advanced knowledge significantly since the early part of the century. The benefits of that progress affect the family, and permeate into numerous fields including human ecology, family medicine and wellness, education, law, psychology, child development and the social sciences. Family research is used by virtually every person or organization or business which interacts with children or markets products to them or their parents.

Over the long haul, however, it is usually the parent who remains in charge of the well-being of children and thus, through that dominance will shape the world for the next generation. The growth and development of children is ever on the parent's mind. But the work of transmitting parental values and guiding children has become more difficult, more troubling for this generation of parents. It is not that children have changed. It is that the world is drastically different from a generation ago.

Parents today are in a powerful struggle – the forces of the environment cascade around their children. It's the sharp rocks under the cascade which are causing difficulty - AIDS, bigotry, violence, substance abuse, the devaluing of human life and immorality. Parents strive to do well – in the tough job of raising children – with varying degrees of skill and competency. They exert tremendous time and energy in rearing children. When they are in the thick of the struggle they realize how hard, how painful and how enduring parenthood is.

Many parents grow through parenting, realizing its joyful, endearing times, happy in the immense challenge of assuming responsibility for the progress of civilization inherent in their task.

Growing and empowering are what this book is all about. By growth and empowerment I mean that through the information, references and support services found in these pages, parents can build on their own skills and knowledge. They can broaden their networks to overcome feelings of individual or family isolation and become more involved in successful interaction with the other institutions in society. They can feel, because they have gained knowledge and information, that they are more able to influence people and organizations which affect their family life.

Virtually all parents are competent. If they function poorly during certain periods, it is because social structures and lack of resources make it impossible for their existing competencies to operate. This book is meant to help parents become more competent; to help them mobilize their resources, thus strengthening family functioning.

In addition, schools, government, cultural, religious, social and judicial institutions, health care services, the entertainment industry and business should not ignore the importance of the family. Each of these institutions has a responsibility to reach out to families and help the family to function well. This helps the primary institution – the family – to raise children who will thrive, prosper and grow.

The strength of all of society's institutions must be applied to providing the social, psychological and economic climate in which to rear children. Parents alone cannot raise a healthy, moral and social child as a solo undertaking. The future viability of our nation will be almost wholly dependent on today's children.

The Michigan PTA, with its 70 years of service to children and schools, understands the crucial role families play in shaping the nation's future. The *Detroit Free Press* understands this too, because its pages reflect changing family demography.

The Michigan PTA Parents' Answer Book is the result of the cooperation and support of the Michigan PTA and the *Detroit Free Press*. This book is brought to you through the efforts of more than 50 professionals in disciplines related to families. Great cooperation and care have been given by these professionals in answering the questions of parents: adolescent suicide, arts education, attention deficit disorder, divorce, drug abuse, discipline, death, homework, parent-teacher conferences, rock music, peer pressure, stepparenting, sex education, separation anxiety, smoking, self-esteem, science education, and the influence, both good and bad, of TV. Painstaking research has identified hundreds of resources and references and placed them in an easy-to-use format, directly after each answer. Such a wealth of resources, on so many issues of concern to parents, is rarely available.

I am grateful to the parents who asked the questions, to the *Detroit Free Press* for encouraging me to find the answers, to the professionals whose long years of study and experience provided such humane and caring answers, and to the Michigan PTA for understanding the importance of both the questions – and the answers.

When parents recognize how competent they really are, and when institutions work together, we can envision a civilization with fewer rocks in the environmental stream to impede the development of children. And we can look for a brighter tomorrow for children and their families today.

I *extend my grateful and heart-felt thanks to the Detroit Free Press, the Michigan PTA, the Advisory Board and guest contributors from the Detroit Free Press, Parent Talk Page; to the Pepsi Cola Company for its support; to Bess Kypros and the Baldwin Public Library staff for their research assistance; to my devoted-to-parents colleagues, Pat Peart and Marcia Danner; and to friends and family who encouraged us,*

Alice R. McCarthy, Ph.D.
Executive Editor

Home-School Connection

Parenting and Family Life

Contemporary Issues

To Michigan's children,
parents and teachers

Alice R. McCarthy, Ph.D.
Director, Detroit Free Press
Parent Talk Page Advisory Board.
President, Bridge Communications;
President, Center for the
Advancement of the Family.
Birmingham, MI

Patricia Peart, B.F.A, B.S.
"What's New" Columnist,
Detroit Free Press.
Art Educator, Graphic Designer
and Publisher of family-related
materials.
Royal Oak, MI

Evelyn Petersen, M.A.
"Teen Talk" and "Parent Talk"
Columnist, Detroit Free Press.
Broadcaster, Educator and
Consultant in early childhood and
parenting.
Traverse City, MI

Louise Reid Ritchie, Ph.D.
"Family Ties" Columnist
Detroit Free Press.
Clinical psychologist, Lecturer
and Consultant on substance
abuse and family issues.
Southfield, MI

John Abbey, B.S.
Total Health Care Coordinator
Ford Motor Company
Dearborn, MI

Y. Gladys Barsamian, J.D.
Judge, Wayne County Juvenile Court
Detroit, MI

E. Bryce Alpern, M.D.
Pediatrician
Children's Hospital of Michigan
Detroit, MI

Scott Bassett, J.D.
Chairperson, Family Law Section
State Bar of Michigan
Victor, Robbins, Bassett
Birmingham, MI

Mira Bakhle, M.S., MACSW
*Parent Educator, Human
Development Specialist*
Child Development Center
Southfield Public Schools
Consultant's Clinic, Southfield, MI

K. Noelle Clark, Ph.D.
Clinical Psychologist
President, Clark & Associates
Southfield, MI

Donald Davis, MSW
Clinical Director
Central Diagnostic & Referral Center
Detroit Health Department
Detroit, MI

Rev. Robert O. Dulin, Jr., M.Div.
Pastor
The Metropolitan Church of God
Detroit, MI

John Dorsey, M.D.
Pediatrician
Birmingham, MI
William Beaumont Hospital
Royal Oak, MI

Joseph Fischoff, M.D.
Director, Psychiatry and Psychology
Children's Hospital of Michigan
Professor & Director, Child &
Adolescent Psychiatry
Wayne State University
School of Medicine, Detroit, MI

Marilyn Droz, M.S.
Director, Council for Children's
Television and the Media
West Bloomfield, MI
Teacher
Royal Oak Public Schools

Bradley S. Greenberg, Ph.D.
Professor & Chair
Department of Telecommunications
Michigan State University
E. Lansing, MI

Melvin Guyer, Ph.D.,J.D.
Associate Professor
Department of Psychiatry &
Psychology
Director, Family and the Law program
University of Michigan, Ann Arbor, MI

Leonard Kaplan, Ed.D.
Professor
College of Education,
Wayne State University
Detroit, MI

Rev. Oscar J. Ice, Ed.M., M.Div.
Director of Interfaith Program
Greater Detroit Interfaith Round Table
Pastor, Evangelical Lutheran Church
in America, Detroit, MI

Dorothy Kispert, M.A.
Project Director, PACT
(Parents and Children Together)
Wayne State University
Detroit, MI

Neil Kalter, Ph.D.
Director, University Center for the
Child & Family, Associate Professor,
Department of Psychology &
Psychiatry
University of Michigan, Ann Arbor, MI

Guadalupe G. Lara, MSW
Certified Pediatric Social Worker
Children's Hospital of Michigan
Detroit, MI

Marlynn Levin, M.A.
Director of Program Development
The Merrill-Palmer Institute for Family
& Human Development Research
Wayne State University, Detroit, MI

Carol Mitchell, Ph.D.
Clinical Psychologist
Resources for Development
Grosse Pointe Woods, MI

Ilona Milke, M.A.
Former Prevention Coordinator
Office of Substance Abuse Services
Michigan Department of
Public Health, Lansing, MI

Dennis Nordmoe, M.Div., M.A.
Supervisor/Program Development
Bureau of Substance Abuse
Department of Health
Detroit, MI

Helene Mills, Ed.D.
Principal
Derby Middle School
Birmingham, MI

Gerryann Olson, Ph.D.
Director of Family Education
Judson Center
Royal Oak, MI

Paul Pearsall, Ph.D.
Author, Former Director
Problems of Daily Living Clinic
Sinai Hospital
W. Bloomfield, MI

Janet Rosen, Ph.D.
Director, Learning Plus
Farmington, MI
Learning Specialist
Detroit Country Day School
Birmingham, MI

Virginia Hill Rice, Ph.D., R.N., C.S.
Associate Professor
Wayne State University
College of Nursing
Detroit, MI

Patricia Ryan, Ph.D.
Professor and Administrative Director
Institute for the Study of Children & Families
Eastern Michigan University
Ypsilanti, MI

Arthur Robin, Ph.D.
Chief of Psychology
Children's Hospital of Michigan
Detroit, MI

Eli Saltz, Ph.D.
Director
The Merrill-Palmer Institute for Family & Human Development Research
Wayne State University, Detroit, MI

Anne K. Soderman, Ph.D.
Associate Professor
Department of Family & Child
Ecology
Michigan State University
East Lansing, MI

Charles C. Vincent, M.D.
Associate Professor, OB-GYN
Wayne State University
School of Medicine
Detroit, MI

Steven Spector, Ph.D.
Licensed Psychologist
Beacon Hill Clinic, Birmingham, MI
Assistant Professor of Pediatrics
Wayne State University, Detroit, MI

David Weikart, Ph.D.
President
High Scope Educational Research
Foundation
Ypsilanti, MI

Rep. Debbie Stabenow, M.S.
State Representative - 58th District
Lansing, MI

T. Berry Brazelton, M.D.
Chief of Child Development Unit
The Children's Hospital, Boston, MA
Professor of Pediatrics
Harvard Medical School, Boston, MA

John Condry, Ph.D.
*Professor of Human Development &
Family Studies*
Cornell University, Ithaca, NY

Cinda-Sue Davis, Ph.D.
Director, Women in Science Program
University of Michigan, Ann Arbor, MI

James Graves, M.D.
Director
Oakland County Community Mental
Health Services Board, Pontiac, MI

Thomas J. Herbst, M.S.
Headmaster
Kensington Academy
Bloomfield Hills, MI

Wanda Jubb, Ed.D.
*Coordinator, Comprehensive School
Health & Physical Education*
Michigan Department of Education
Lansing, MI

Katherine H. Mills, Ph.D.
Clinical Psychologist
Supervisor of Psychological Services
Michigan Osteopathic
Medical Center-Adult Mental Health
Detroit, MI

Ann Weeks Moye, Ph.D.
Licensed Psychologist
Midwestern Educational Resources
Center, Inc., Bloomfield Hills, MI

Herbert S. Moyer, Ed.D.
Superintendent of Education
Bedford Public Schools
Temperance, MI

Harry E. Pike, Ph.D.
Executive Vice President
Lake Superior State University
Sault Ste. Marie, MI

Meri K. Pohutsky, M.A.
Director, The Sanctuary
Shelter for Runaways
Royal Oak, MI

Joy Schumacher, R.N.
*Program Coordinator, AIDS
Prevention and Control*
Oakland County Health Division
Pontiac, MI

Patricia T. Siegel, Ph.D.
Director of Psychology Training
Children's Hospital of Michigan
Detroit, MI

Donald B. Sweeney, M.A.
Coordinator, School Health Programs
Center for Health Promotion
Michigan Department of Public
Health, Lansing, MI

Cledie C. Taylor, Ph.D.
Assistant Director
Children's Museum
Detroit Public Schools
Detroit, MI

Robert West, Ph.D.
Director
Cranbrook Institute of Science
Bloomfield Hills, MI

Marilyn L. Wheaton
Executive Director
Concerned Citizens for the Arts in
Michigan
Michigan Advocates for the Arts
Detroit, MI

Home-School Connection

Q Neither my husband nor I are the least bit artistic, but we have a gnawing feeling that we should not only be expanding our own interest in the arts, but also be thinking about some type of art experience for our children. But where do we start with kids already 7 and 9, who are into scouts, sports and TV?

A **The arts are a part of life in all healthy societies.** Art forms are infinitely varied and our active relation to them can take place in many ways. Art need not be an "add-on" in your lives and in the lives of your young scouts, sports and TV enthusiasts. It might rather take the form of a shift in attitude, an expanded notion of what is fun or a new way to spend quiet time together.

Even if you can't draw a straight line, you can make observations about what pleases you visually. You can share comments such as "the lines of the new Ford Probe are very pleasing" or "I have selected this color for the den because it makes the room look warm and comfortable." This will signal to the children that art elements such as line, color and shape are a normal and acceptable part of being. In truth, children's awareness and taste are usually a reflection of their parents'.

The whole family might enjoy going to an arts festival where there is something to do for everyone. Take along a bit of plaster to the beach and cast some found or sand-constructed object. Bring into your home a musical instrument – perhaps a guitar or a wooden flute. Find an alternative TV program where the arts and artists are introduced and explained. Ask the most likely sibling to plan entertainment for a family backyard picnic. Everyone could get involved with a story, a song or acrobatic feat...if you don't think these activities are silly, the children won't either.

Some paper and crayons in the back seat on even a short trip can be good for all. Encourage a family member to make a sign for the yard sale or wherever the need might be. If there is a church or community childrens' choir, hear it and join it. Seek out gallery and museum exhibitions, dance classes, theatre groups or concerts just to make the art community familiar to the whole family. The children may ask for more involvement, but even if they do not, their sensitivity to the art arena will be increased, they will know more of the their own abilities and be more open to other ways of seeing, doing and knowing.

Your local arts council will be able to assist you with schedules for festivals in your area, as well as direct you to corporations which have art collections to see. The entertainment section of your daily paper as well as local magazines will give theatre, concert and exhibit schedules.

Cledie Taylor

|A| **The arts provide children with a means for expression and communication.** Painting, music, dance and drama communicate thoughts and feelings through visual forms, sounds and movement.

The arts can produce tremendous pleasure, and things that give us pleasure usually motivate us. A child's behavior can be affected enormously by the arts, particularly in the areas of motivation and discipline.

Creating an image on a canvas or a piece of paper, molding an object, moving the body to sound, acting out a script, or writing poetic thoughts provide children with a sense of accomplishment and pride and motivate them to do more, to be better. The arts are essential in young people's lives if they are to grow up to be imaginative thinkers, if they are to be leaders with creative, inventive minds. The arts, through creative expression, give children self-confidence, allowing them to be productive and assertive.

A child who expresses a desire to participate in an art form ought to be encouraged and nurtured. No monetary value can be placed on a child's future. Money spent on art training, whether it be painting lessons or some other form of creative learning, is money well spent, an investment in a child's future.

Marilyn L. Wheaton

Resources

▲ **Concerned Citizens for the Arts in Michigan**
350 Madison Avenue, Suite 503, Detroit 48226
(313) 961-1776

▲ **Michigan Council for the Arts**
Provides information and schedules of arts events and activities.
1200 Sixth Street, Detroit, MI 48226-2461
(313) 256-3731

■ *Michigan Travel Events*
A calendar of festivals, performing arts and special events.
Michigan Travel Bureau, P.O. Box 30226, Lansing, MI 48909
☎ Or call toll-free 1-800-5432-YES

■ **Young Audiences of Michigan**
Non-profit, community outreach service providing professional performances and workshops for groups of students throughout the state.
(313) 843-6940

✔ **Arts classes** for children are available through local art associations, art museums, school district community education programs, city recreation departments and other community and arts organizations.
Orchestras, theatre groups and museums (including the Detroit Institute of Arts, Detroit Symphony Orchestra and the Michigan Opera Theatre) have outreach programs that bring performances and workshops to schools. In many cases, financial aid is available to help schools underwrite the cost.

❑ *Creative Art for Learning* by Merle B. Karnes
(Council for Exceptional Children, Reston, VA, 1979, $8.00)

❑ *Developing Talent in Young People* by Benjamen S. Bloom
(Ballantine Books, 1985, $9.95)

❑ *Doing Art Together* by Murial Silberstein
(Simon and Schuster, 1983, $12.95)

Q My child does not seem to be college material. How important is it for her to go to college? Is getting a good job dependent on going to a certain school?

A Unfortunately, our society has overemphasized college education. Many students enter college and struggle for years. They struggle for a career choice, never really finding a job that makes them happy.

College isn't for everyone. There are many types of colleges that should be considered, including community colleges and specialty education programs.

Parents can help their child by pointing out that where one goes to school is much less important than what he or she learns. What a person learns depends on experiences, people with whom they relate, teachers they are exposed to, and willingness to broaden their horizons for career choice.

If we focus on the name of the university, we miss the point that learning is becoming aware of the mysteries within. We must learn to look inward for an education – as much as we look outward. The only name that matters on a diploma is the student's name, and the only education that matters is one that prepares a person for a career that brings happiness and joy to the worker and those he or she is working for.

Paul Pearsall

Resources

❏ *College – Yes or No?* by William F. Shanahan
(Arco Publishing, Div. of Prentice-Hall, 1983, $7.95)

■ *Career World,* a magazine with information on different occupations.
Published monthly, September - May.
Single subscriptions $12.50 per year prepaid; lower for multiple copies.
General Learning Corp., 60 Revere Dr., Northbrook, Il 60062
(312) 564-4070

Q Our son is a junior in high school and will need financial aid to attend college. How can we find out about scholarships and financial assistance programs?

A There are four major sources of financial aid: the federal government, the State of Michigan, the individual institution, and a wide variety of private sources. The criteria for awarding each form of aid varies. Merit-based aid is awarded solely on the basis of the student's academic performance. Need-based aid is determined by the student's family financial situation and by the cost of the institution the student wishes to attend.

To determine the amount of need-based eligibility, the student must complete a financial statement. The **Financial Aid Form (FAF)** or the **Family Financial Statement (FFS)** are used by most students applying for need-based aid in Michigan. The forms are completed after January 1st of the senior year. Colleges and universities may have different deadlines for receiving information from the FAF or FFS, so it is important to check the institution of choice to determine its deadline.

The federal government offers aid to students through a combination of grant programs, work-study programs and loan programs. Grants are awards that do not need to be repaid. Work-study offers students the chance to work and earn money while in school, and loans are borrowed money that must be repaid with interest. Most federal programs are need-based.

The State of Michigan offers a combination of scholarship, grant, work and loan programs. Eligibility for the competitive scholarship is based on ACT test scores and financial need. Students must take the ACT no later than the October examination date during their senior year. The Michigan Tuition Grant Program is available to students attending private

---

colleges and universities in Michigan with the amount of the grant variable depending upon need and cost. The Michigan work study program is funded by the state and allocated to eligible institutions.

Most colleges and universities have institutional grant and scholarship programs. Most are either merit-based or need-based or some combination of the two. Merit scholarships are awarded on the basis of the student's high school academic performance, ACT or SAT scores, class standing or some combination of these factors. Financial need is not a factor in these awards. Some scholarships are awarded according to academic performance, but the amount of the scholarship is determined by the student's financial need. Colleges and universities also offer scholarships donated to the institution by private donors. The criteria for these scholarships vary widely, according to the criteria established by the donor.

Service organizations, places of business and private donors within virtually every community in the state also sponsor scholarships available to students from that community. The high school counselor is the best source of information regarding these private scholarships. Once awarded, most of these scholarships can be used at the institution of the student's choice.

Parents and students should begin investigating sources of assistance early in the senior year of high school. In addition to assistance from high school counselors and financial aid offices, most areas of the state will offer a financial aid workshop during the fall months for prospective students and their parents. The earlier the aid application process is begun, the better the chances will be of receiving assistance.

Harry Pike

Resources

✓ **Michigan Education Trust**
Department of Treasury, P. O. Box 30198, Lansing, MI 48909
800-638-4543, 8-6 M-F

✓ *College Handbook* ($15.95) is published annually by The College Board, a non-profit membership organization of 2,600 colleges, universities and education associations, providing a variety of tests for achievement, placement and financial aid. The College Board has many other resources available, including computer software, to assist college-bound students. Check with your school counseling office or write to:
College Board Publications, Box 886, New York, NY 10106

❑ **"Who Says You Can't,"** from the Michigan Department of Education, is available at most high school counseling offices. Lists types of financial aid.

✎ **"Getting the Most Out of High School:** Tips on College Planning" is free from your high school counseling office or from
Michigan Department of Education, Student Financial Assistance Service,
P.O. Box 30008, Lansing, MI 48909
(Other free fact sheets on financial assistance available.)

✎ **"Need a Lift to Educational Opportunities, Careers, Loans, Scholarships and Employment?"** (34th edition, American Legion., $1.00)
Check with your local American Legion post or write:
American Legion National Emblem Sales
P.O. Box 1050, Indianapolis, IN 46206

✎ **"Student Guide: Five Federal Financial Aid Programs"** and application for Federal Student Aids (free)
Federal Student Aid Program, Dept. DEA-086, Pueblo, CO 81009

❑ *Don't Miss Out: The Ambitious Student's Guide to Financial Aid* ($4.50)
Octamerm Associates
P.O. Box 3437, Alexandria, VA 22302-9990

❑ *Twelve Winning Ways to College Admission*
by Howard Greene and Robert Minton (Little, Brown, 1987, $12.50)

Q How does the Michigan Education Trust (MET) work? We are a middle-class family with two children to put through college. The MET may be good for our younger son, but our older son is already a junior in high school. It is possible to purchase a contract for the older boy?

A The Michigan Education Trust (MET) is a program that would enable parents, grandparents, or anyone else to guarantee a child's Michigan college tuition by allowing them to pre-purchase tuition for a fixed predetermined amount. The trust then guarantees the cost of all four years of undergraduate tuition at any public Michigan college, community college or university. Purchasers can make a one-time-only payment or periodic payments anytime after the birth of the child. The trust will invest the money and the interest earned will cover the tuition when the child needs it. Payments are made to a financial institution through a loan process.

Based on today's cost for four years' tuition at Michigan colleges, the current estimate for a one-time lump sum payment for a newborn is $6,800 depending on options chosen. The cost increases with the age of the child.

Several refund options and limited transfer options will be be available if the child decides not to enter college. If a child wants to go to an independent college, the tuition payment will be made up to the weighted tuition for public four-year colleges. This means somewhat higher than average tuition.

Interest earnings will be exempt from the purchaser's federal and state taxes, and purchasers can also deduct their contribution to the trust from their Michigan-taxable income.

There is no age limit – parents are even using MET for their college-age children. Watch your newspapers for announcements regarding the next opportunity to apply.

Evelyn Petersen

Basic Federal Aid Programs

The federal government provides billions of dollars in aid to college students, under five basic programs. Students may apply for any combination of these grants and loans on their financial aid forms:

Pell Grants: Awarded to undergraduates only, the Pell Grant is based on need, cost of education, enrollment status (full or part-time) and length of attendance. The maximum Pell Grant for the 1988-89 academic year was $2,200.

Supplemental Educational Opportunity Grant: Geared to undergraduates from low-income families, students can receive a grant for up to $4,000 a year, depending on need. Each campus receives a set amount of money for SEOGs, and when the money is gone, no more awards can be made that year.

Work-study: This program provides jobs to undergraduate and graduate students for educational expenses. Students earn minimum wage or more depending on the job. Eligibility is determined by financial need, and the amount of aid awarded from other sources. The employer -- often the university -- pays 20 percent of the wage and the federal government 80 percent.

Perkins Loan (formerly National Direct Student Loan): This is a loan with a five percent interest rate for graduate and undergraduate students. Eligibility is based on need and availability of money. Undergraduates borrow an amount up to the yearly maximum set by individual institutions. The debt for undergraduate and graduate degrees combined cannot exceed $18,000. Repayment begins six months after graduation and students can take up to 10 years. Generally minimum payments are $30 a month.

Guaranteed Student Loan: Through financial institutions, students can get a loan based on need of up to $2,625 a year for the first two years of undergraduate work, $4,000 a year for the remaining years and $7,500 a year for graduate work. The interest rate for new borrowers is eight percent. The total allowable outstanding debt is $17,250 for undergraduate students, $54,750 for graduates. Repayment begins six to 12 months after graduation, depending on the interest rate. Students have up to five years to repay the loans.

A related program is the **Parents Loan for Undergraduate Students** and **Supplemental Loans for Students.** The 10-12 percent loans are limited to $4,000 a year, with no test for need. Applications are available through various lenders including Manufacturers Bank and National Bank of Detroit.

From the 1988 Detroit Free Press Michigan College Guide

Q **I'm appalled at the difference in requirements for my son's driver's education classes as compared to his sister's 10 years ago. All he's done is drive a new automatic car for about five hours. What are some things we can watch for or do as we ride with him to give him the extra help and experience he needs?**

A **New drivers really need about 25 hours of supervised driving, and they get only five or six hours in most driver's education classes. Parents must make up the difference.**

Ride with your son and ask yourself these questions: Does he look well ahead and to the sides? Does he check to see what's behind? Does he always let others know what he is going to do? Does he drift out of the driving lane? Does he swing out too far when turning? Does he always wear seat belts (Do you? Youngsters will copy their parents.)? Does he come to a full stop at stop signs?

Does your son drive according to speed limits, matching speed to road conditions, and does he follow at a safe distance (not easy for impatient teenagers)? Try to get teens to start trips 10 minutes earlier when they're driving so they won't rush. (You can demonstrate that one, too.) Finally, does your son agree that driving and drinking do not mix?

Parents must set the conditions under which teens can drive. This includes things like trip lengths, number of trips, driving at night, going to "new" places on new roads, bad weather driving, and what passengers they can carry.

Discuss your conditions with your son. Make sure he understands your reason for rules, and that these are based on facts and experience as well as your concern for him. As teens improve their driving, be sure to modify your conditions so they are rewarded for being responsible. More careful driving will mean more privileges.

Evelyn Petersen

A You are fortunate that your youngster has had 5 hours behind the wheel of a car, even though that time is not nearly adequate and you will need to drive with your youngster.

Dick Claflin, Michigan Department of Education Driver's Education consultant, tells me that the driver's ed program taught in Michigan by 630 public, private and commercial programs does not require that youngsters have specific training before appearing at the Secretary of State's office for a permit. The Department of Education has 97 classroom objectives in driver's education and 30 skills for driver performance. If your youngster can pass tests to prove he has the knowledge and skills to drive a car, he can go immediately to obtain his temporary permit.

This program was established several years ago to reduce a tight Michigan budget. In addition, small schools in rural Michigan found the six hours behind the wheel and 30 classroom hours repetitive and expensive to administer. Some rural youngsters learn to drive early.

Currently the State Board of Education is conducting an in-depth study to determine if cutting back on behind-the-wheel time, road-time and classroom instruction is resulting in more accidents.

Call Mr. Claflin at (517) 373-3314 with your concerns.

Alice R. McCarthy

Resources

■ **"Parents,"** a free booklet from:
Bureau of Driver Improvement, Post Licensing Control Division
Michigan Department of State, Lansing, MI 48918

■ **"New Drivers, A Parent's Guide"**
Usually distributed in driver's education classes, this pamphlet is also available free from:
Traffic Safety Association of Michigan
122 S. Grand Ave., Suite 215, Lansing, MI 48933

Q I've been told that my child is "gifted." What does this mean and what should I do about it?

A A common misconception is that "gifted" merely means having an above average IQ. The definition is far more complex. The official definition, adopted by the Michigan Advisory Council for Gifted and Talented, is:

Gifted and talented children means children, and whenever applicable, youth, who are identified at the preschool, elementary or secondary level, as possessing demonstrated or potential abilities that give evidence of high performance capability in areas such as intellectual, creative, specific academic or leadership ability, or in the performing and visual arts, and who, by reason thereof, require services or activities not ordinarily provided by the school.

Talent and giftedness, therefore, are not necessarily limited to a child's overall ability to perform above grade level in an academic setting.

As all children differ in their area of giftedness or talent, so do characteristics applicable to them. It is rare to find a child with all the characteristics listed below. Since giftedness may occur in many different areas, it is difficult to compile one short list of all the traits that may be present, and this is by no means a complete list! Some characteristics are diametrically opposed, tending to confuse identification of these youngsters even more. In general, all children have some characteristics present, but the gifted and talented usually exhibit more of them, at an earlier age.

Gifted and talented children:

Typically learn to read earlier and with better comprehension.

Commonly learn basic skills better, more quickly and with less practice.

Commonly take less for granted, wanting to know "how" and "why."

Typically sustain longer periods of concentration and attention than their peers.

Frequently seem to have endless energy, which is often misdiagnosed as "hyperactivity."

Often prefer the company of older children and adults.

Show keen powers of observation.

Often read a great deal on their own.

Often appear to be daydreaming.

Consistently have superior scores on standardized tests.

May show an intense interest in a particular area.

Will have widely varied interests and be knowledgeable about many things.

Have well-developed powers of abstraction, conceptualization and synthesizing abilities.

Have well-developed common sense.

Have a well-developed sense of humor.

Have a highly developed moral and ethical sense.

Have a well-developed sense of self and a realistic idea of their capabilities and potential.

May try to hide their abilities so as not to "stick out."

Approximately 3 to 5 percent of the population falls into the gifted and talented area. Identification has been inadequate in the past, partly because there is such a broad range of talent and giftedness that there is no one single tool which identifies all such children.

The more tools used to identify the gifted and talented, the more accurate the assessment will be. Some commonly used tools include: teacher nomination/observation, parent interviews, biographical sketches of the child by the parents, autobiographical inventories, peer nominations, case studies IQ Tests (Stanford-Binet and/or Wechsler-revised) with minimum scores of 125-135 generally required, and the Torrance Test of Creative Thinking.

At the same time, specialized tests need to be developed and employed to identify the culturally diverse gifted and talented, such as children from Black American, Native American, Mexican American, Asian American and Puerto Rican populations. Some possibilities are the Raven Progressive Matrices and Renzulli-Hartman Communication Characteristics.

Special identification criteria are also required for the gifted and talented handicapped child which remove the mask that a disability can place over intellectual ability, talent and creativity.

Every child is entitled to an education which meets his or her needs. They should neither be bored nor frustrated; they should not be asked to settle for less than what they are capable of doing, just as no student should be frustrated by being required to perform at a level beyond his ability.

The curriculum for the gifted and talented should include the development of abstract thinking, the sharpening of reasoning abilities, practice in creative problem solving and higher cognitive processing.

Some of the ways school districts are accommodating the needs of the gifted and talented are through enrichment programs, acceleration, mentorships, individualized education programs, cluster grouping (within a regular classroom), self-contained classrooms and magnet schools.

Gifted students are first and foremost children. Their needs must be met educationally, socially and psychologically. As students, they are entitled to an education that matches their peers in appropriateness.

Michigan PTA

Resources

▲ **Michigan Association for the Academically Talented, Inc.**
P.O. Box 16007, Lansing, MI 48901

▲ **Nancy Mincemoyer, Gifted and Talented Consultant**
Michigan Department of Education, P.O. Box 30008, Lansing, MI 48909

▲ **American Association for Gifted Children, Inc.**
15 Gramercy Park, New York, NY 10003

▲ **National Association for Gifted Children**
4175 Lovell Rd., Suite 140, Circle Pines, MN 55014
(612) 784-3475

▲ **Office of Gifted and Talented**
U.S. Department of Education, Washington, D.C. 20001

❏ *Bringing Out the Best: A Resource and Guide for Parents of Young Gifted Children* by J. Saunders and P. Espel
(Free Spirit Publishers, 1986, $12.95)

❏ *Enjoy Your Gifted Child* by C.A. Takacs
(Syracuse University Press, 1986, $12.95)

❏ *Guiding the Gifted Child* by James T. Webb, et al
(Ohio Psychology, 1987, $12.95)

❏ *It's O.K. to be Gifted or Talented! A Parent/Child Manual by Joel Engel (TOR, 1987, $12.95)*

❏ *Parenting the Gifted: Developing the Promise*
by Sheila C. Perino and Joseph Perino
(R.R. Bowker Company, 1981, $14.95)

❏ *Parents' Guide to Raising a Gifted Child: Recognizing and Developing Your Child's Potential* by J . Alvino (Little, Brown & Co., 1986, $19.95)

❏ *The Gifted and Talented Catalogue* by Susan Amerikaner and Sarina Simon (Price Stern Sloan, 1988, $10.95)

❏ *The Gifted Kids Survival Guide* for ages 7-12 by Judy Galbraith
(Free Spirit Publishing, 1987, $7.95)
The Gifted Kids Survival Guide II for ages 11-18 ($9.95)

❏ *Underachievement Syndrome: Causes and Cures* by Sylvia Rimm
(Apple Pub. WISC, 1986, $15.00)

■ *Gifted Children Monthly,* Dr. J. Alvino, Editor-in-Chief (11 issues, $25.00)
P.O. Box 10149, Des Moines, IA 50340
(609) 582-0277

■ *Roeper Review* (quarterly, $25.00)
P.O. Box 329, Bloomfield Hills, MI 48013; (313) 642-1500

Q How much health education do our children receive in school, and what does it cover?

A The Michigan Model for Comprehensive School Health Education, a curriculum for Michigan school children, provides approximately 40 lessons per grade level from K-6 and approximately 50 lessons per grade level 7-8. Ten broad health topics are covered: community health, consumer health, emotional and mental health, family health, growth and development, disease prevention and control, nutrition, personal health practices, safety, and substance use and abuse.

Each year the Michigan Model curriculum builds sequentially to provide health-oriented knowledge, attitudes and skills necessary to promote and maintain health over a child's lifetime. Subjects in the areas of mental and physical health include stress management, nutrition needs, dental care, effects of drugs and consumer health problems. Life skill competencies such as decision-making and problem-solving abilities – resisting peer pressure and developing a sense of self-esteem and success – are also included.

Parents are encouraged to become involved in providing a broad-based foundation for healthy decision-making. Information handouts and exercises are provided for parents to use at home to reinforce learning at school. Parents are also encouraged to assist in the classroom.

Currently, the Michigan Model for Comprehesive School Health Education is a cooperative effort of the Michigan Department of Education, Michigan Department of Public Health, Michigan Department of Mental Health, Michigan Department of Social Services, Office of Substance Abuse Services, Office of Health and Medical Affairs and Office of Highway Safety Planning. The model is an award-winner. We are pleased to make it available to Michigan youngsters!

Wanda H. Jubb

✔ **Contact Dr. Wanda Jubb, Michigan Department of Education**
P.O. Box 30008, Lansing, MI 48909
(517) 373-2589
Dr. Jubb is responsible for coordinating delivery of this curriculum
state-wide. Also be in touch with your Intermediate School District office
(listed under your county in your local telephone directory.) Your child's
teacher may need volunteers to reinforce this health education, so let your
school know if you can help.

Q **How much should we help our children with homework?**

A Give them as much help as they seem to need. Don't do the work for them, but show them some of the best ways to complete the task.

Teach your children how to use resources such as the library. If you don't know the answer, don't be ashamed. Find people and places that can help both of you find the information you need.

Let your child complete the assignment, then review it and make constructive suggestions.

With your child, discuss the best time and place to do homework.

If your child has difficulties with homework, encourage him or her to talk to the teacher.

Children must take responsibility for their own behavior. Help them understand the values and benefits of accomplishment. Don't bribe, threaten, nag or punish. Help them understand the consequences of incomplete assignments.

Let them know you love them whether they do their homework or not.

Marlynn Levin

A How involved you get with actual homework assignments depends on your children's grades and achievements. Usually the younger the child, the more guidance is needed.

Elementary school students often need extra help. If your child has been given a work sheet, for example, make sure the child understands the directions. Do the first few together, then watch your child do the next problem or two.

When your child is finished, check the assignment. Praise correct answers and point out errors so they can be corrected.

In the upper grades, you may become less involved with daily assignments, but you still need to know what's expected. Meet each of your child's teachers and ask what kind of assignments will be given. When your school sponsors an open house, make a point to attend. Teachers frequently describe what they'll cover in their courses and their homework policies during an open house.

National PTA

Resources

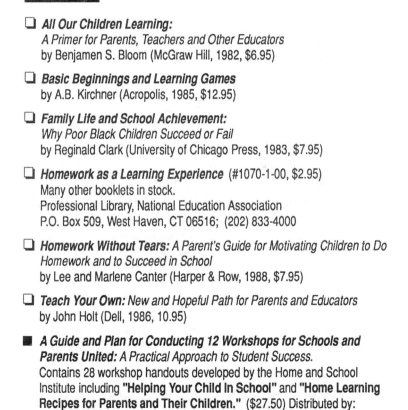

❏ *All Our Children Learning:*
A Primer for Parents, Teachers and Other Educators
by Benjamen S. Bloom (McGraw Hill, 1982, $6.95)

❏ *Basic Beginnings and Learning Games*
by A.B. Kirchner (Acropolis, 1985, $12.95)

❏ *Family Life and School Achievement:*
Why Poor Black Children Succeed or Fail
by Reginald Clark (University of Chicago Press, 1983, $7.95)

❏ *Homework as a Learning Experience* (#1070-1-00, $2.95)
Many other booklets in stock.
Professional Library, National Education Association
P.O. Box 509, West Haven, CT 06516; (202) 833-4000

❏ *Homework Without Tears: A Parent's Guide for Motivating Children to Do Homework and to Succeed in School*
by Lee and Marlene Canter (Harper & Row, 1988, $7.95)

❏ *Teach Your Own: New and Hopeful Path for Parents and Educators*
by John Holt (Dell, 1986, 10.95)

■ *A Guide and Plan for Conducting 12 Workshops for Schools and Parents United: A Practical Approach to Student Success.*
Contains 28 workshop handouts developed by the Home and School Institute including **"Helping Your Child In School"** and **"Home Learning Recipes for Parents and Their Children."** ($27.50) Distributed by: National Education Association. P.O. 509, West Haven, CT 06516 (202) 833-4000.

Homework Hints

▲ Check to see that your children understand assignments. If there is a problem, work through an example with them.

▲ Sign and date your young children's homework. Teachers appreciate it when they know that the parents are interested enough to check over their children's homework and see that it is finished.

▲ Follow up on homework assignments by asking to see your children's homework after it has been returned by the teacher. Look at the teacher's comments to see if your children have done the assignments correctly.

▲ Contact the teacher if you don't understand the assignments or your child has a special problem. This is a common problem among parents, so don't hesitate to contact the teacher.

▲ Look for homework daily. Assume that your children have homework to do every day.

▲ Resist doing your children's homework for them. Work with them and encourage them to do the work themselves.

▲ Try to be home and available during homework time so that your children know that you value homework as another part of their education.

▲ Be sure to praise your children for a job well done. Encourage the good work that your children do and comment about improvements they have made.

From "Help Your Child Get the Most Out of Homework" by the National PTA and National Education Association. 1988 © National PTA, NEA

Q How can we decide if our child is ready for kindergarten?

A **Kindergartens differ greatly in their orientations.** Some stress development of social and cognitive skills, while others are essentially versions of first grade.

The following traits are often acquired in kindergarten. However, the child who has many of these skills before starting is most likely to be ready for kindergarten. The child should be able to:

- **spend time away from home and parents and enjoy it;**
- **give and receive information verbally;**
- **show curiosity and positive attitudes toward learning new things;**
- **get pleasure from listening to stories, looking at pictures and telling stories from the pictures of a family book.**

Eli Saltz

A **School readiness is much more than reading readiness. It encompasses the whole child** and is concerned with social, emotional and physical maturity as well as with intellectual ability. Ready children are able to cope comfortably and thus are free to use their intellectual powers.

The first year of school is very important. It is the foundation upon which all other education is built. Placing children in kindergarten before they are mature enough to really profit from the experience may cause them to "shut off" – reject learning – often for 12 years.

When determining school readiness, we must consider sex differences (5-year-old boys are, on the average, six months less mature than 5-year-old girls), social-emotional development, hearing, perception, motor skills and ability to learn concepts, in addition to chronological age, physical size and language skills.

Birmingham, Mich. School District

❑ *Starting School:*
How to Help Your 3 to 8 Year Old Make the Most of School
by Margery Kranyik (Continuum, 1982, $8.95)

✔ Visit your public library and choose books with your child about starting school. Many titles are in print, including:

❑ *Don't Eat Too Much Turkey* by M.. Cohen (Greenwillow, 1987, $11.95)

❑ *I Don't Want to Go to School* by A. Gross
(Childrens Press,1982, $2.95)

❑ *Timothy Goes To School* by R. Wells (Dial, 1981, $7.50)

❑ *I Started School Today* by K. Frandsen (Childrens Press, 1984, $2.95)

❑ *When You Go To Kindergarten* by J. Howe (Knopf, 1986, $5.95)

Parents: A Child's First and Foremost Teachers

With the help and support of their parents, children learn and master an array of physical skills; they learn how to communicate their thoughts, feelings, ideas and desires; and they collect a great many notions and impressions about the events and values of their family's culture – all before they enter preschool.

However, parents often fail to recognize their own contributory role and sometimes think that only classroom teachers "teach." It is important to realize that:

1. Parenting is teaching.

2. As parents you already know a lot about child development in general and about your own children in particular.

3.Teachers are not purveyors of knowledge but rather people who wish to support and extend the learning that's already going on at home.

David Weikart

Q **Is it true that boys are behind girls in their development? What does this mean in terms of our 5-year-old starting kindergarten?**

A **Boys are sometimes more immature than girls in the preschool and elementary years.** They typically catch up and often surpass girls. Things to remember about growing children are:

Children develop at highly individualized rates.

Appreciate your child as an individual.

Your child doesn't need to be a carbon copy of other children.

Girls tend to be more mature in areas of fine motor development, such as handwriting, cutting and pasting.

Boys tend to excel in areas of gross motor development, such as throwing, running and jumping, and mathematics.

Preschool and elementary boys sometimes are more restless and have more difficulty concentrating and sitting still than girls.

Development patterns vary considerably. Growth is often in spurts.

Learning styles of boys and girls are far more alike than different.

A child's attitude toward learning is a more important factor than the sex of the child.

Noelle Clark

A **A "developmental lag" exists between many boys and their female counterparts at an early age.** Boys, more often than girls, may need an extra year in kindergarten before they are ready for the types of learning required in grade school. Once in grade school there are differences which exist among the students in any classroom, and the word "normal" must be broadly interpreted.

Through being associated with an all-boys school that recently went co-ed, I have witnessed the change in attitude about learning differences between boys and girls. Today it is more valid to say that *individual* learning styles vary.

Some traits are more common to one sex than the other, but boys or girls can exhibit a learning style that might more often be found in the opposite sex – and still be perfectly normal.

Thomas Herbst

Resources

❑ *Frames of Mind* by Howard Gardner (Basic Books, 1983, $9.95)

❑ *In Their Own Way:*
  Discovering and Encouraging Your Child's Personal Learning Style
  by Thomas Armstrong (Jeremy P. Tarcher, Inc., 1987, $8.95)

7 Kinds of Intelligence

Harvard psychologist Howard Gardner has received national attention with his theory which defines 7 kinds of intelligence, possessed by everyone in different proportions. These 7 levels are:

▲ **Linquisitic:** auditory and verbal skills; understanding the slight differences in word meanings.

▲ **Logical-Mathematical:** conceptual thinking; the general abilities that traditional IQ tests measure.

▲ **Musical:** comprehension of music as another kind of language expression.

▲ **Bodily-Kinesthetic:** body control and motor skills; process knowledge through physical sensations;

▲ **Interpersonal:** sensitivity and insight to the moods and motives of others.

▲ **Intrapersonal:** insight to one's own feelings; ability to use this knowledge to guide one's actions.

▲ **Spatial:** visual skills; ability to understand, duplicate and manipulate shapes and forms.

Q My child's teacher says that Jimmy, 7, has an "attention deficit disorder." She explained somewhat but I'm not too clear on what is wrong, or what we can do at home to help.

A Attention-Deficit Hyperactivity Disorder (ADHD) is a common problem experienced by many people. It is characterized by being unable to organize and complete work.

Children who have ADHD cannot attend to a set task, are impulsive, over-active and easily distracted. There are so many inconsistent behaviors that an accurate diagnosis is difficult, but comprehensive psychological and educational testing is necessary to determine what is wrong and make corrections.

Teachers report that children with this problem lack organization; assignments are carelessly done, incomplete or not begun. They are restless, fidgety, forgetful and overly talkative. The child may blurt out answers to questions, interrupting the teacher with unrelated thoughts and actions. Talking during quiet time causes the child to be mislabeled as a "troublemaker." Handwriting is tediously done; other eye-hand coordination problems are often present. Learning disabilities are common. Your child may be easily frustrated yet forgive easily.

At home, it is critical that parents be patient, consistent and structured. Decide which behavior change is most important, follow through carefully and predictably. Try to avoid situations where your child can become overly stimulated.

If your pediatrician feels that medication might be helpful, it should be considered. There is a good chance that your child will become happier, learn more easily and get along better. Counseling is also suggested when behavior problems are overly upsetting to your child and others.

Steven Spector

A Children with Attention-Deficit Hyperactivity Disorder (ADHD) frequently experience school failure. Reading and writing require concentration and children with ADHD are uncontrollably drawn to some other activity or sensation, while trying to focus on a specific task.

Children with ADHD also can develop a profile of insecurity, low self-esteem and poor social skills. Low tolerance for frustration and temper outbursts are quite common.

Extensive research is being carried out to find the causes of ADHD but no definite conclusion has yet been reached. There are many reasons for this disorder and there is a tendency for this to run in families. Boys seem to display the symptoms more than girls.

ADHD needs clinical attention. Consult a pediatrician, pediatric psychiatrist, licensed child psychologist, or pediatric neurologist. ADHD can be treated successfully.

Above all, please don't blame yourself for Jimmy's condition, because it is certainly not brought on by faulty parenting.

Mira Bakhle

A I would suggest that you read widely on the subject of Attention-Deficit Hyperactivity Disorder. Understand that your child will require extra time and attention from you and the other adults in his life. Because of this you will be required to become your child's advocate at school and in other activities – helping those adults to understand and work effectively with your child.

Youngsters with this condition tend to encounter more problems in school because of their lessened ability to concentrate or "focus" for an extended period of time. Smaller class size may be an aid, but cannot always be the only criterion for placement. A knowledgeable and sensitive teacher with consistent expectations is a must.

The great tendency at the beginning of a new school year is to "wait and see what happens with the new teacher." If you use this approach, you do so at the risk of wasting at least a month in the education of your child. Rather, be up front. Any teacher worthy of the name needs all the information background on your child that you can offer.

Of course, consult your pediatrician. Be open to a referral to a pediatric neurologist for a definitive assessment. Medication, when specified by physician, can often be a great help to the child.

Thomas Herbst

Resources

▲ **A.D.D. Association of Michigan**
Meets at North Congregational Church
26275 Northwestern Hwy., Southfield
Call Kathie McWhorter (313) 356-5747

■ **Attention Disorder Clinic** at Children's Hospital, Detroit
(313) 745-4000 (Pediatric Clinic), 8-4:30 M-F

❑ *The Hyperactive Child* by Ronald Friedman and Guy T. Doyal
(Inter Print Publishers, 1986, $4.95)

❑ *The Hyperactive Child and the Family: The Complete What-To-Do Handbook* by John F. Taylor (Dodd Publishers, 1987, $6.95)

✔ Also see resources under "Learning Disabilities – The Law."

Q I understand there is a Public Law 94 which makes provisions for the learning disabled. What are these provisions and how can I make sure my child benefits from them?

A Public Law 94-142 is a federal law which provides for diagnostic testing, school placement and remediation in public schools for children who are classified as "learning disabled." A "learning disabled child" has *average or above average intelligence* but is weak in one or more of the following areas: 1) oral expression, 2) listening comprehension, 3) written expression, 4) basic reading skill, 5) mathematics calculation, and 6) mathematics reasoning.

Your child must have a severe discrepancy between his academic achievement and intellectual skills in one or more areas. Schools will provide the multi-disciplinary, diagnostic testing to evaluate the child. The team should include the classroom teacher, the school psychologist, speech pathologist, social worker, learning disabilities teacher and the principal. A planning committee or "IEPC" is called to meet with the parents to discuss the results of testing and to determine if any special placement and curriculum needs to be planned. It will be important that the diagnostic team provide you with a complete written report of the testing and interpretation of these tests. This report should include curriculum recommendations for the teacher, as well as specialists working with your child.

Frequently, parents have to wait many months for the school to provide this testing. Parents sometimes decide to consult outside professionals for an in-depth assessment before the child is enrolled in private tutoring.

Janet Rosen

A Federal law requires that school districts either by themselves or in concert with other districts must make available free and appropriate learning sites for all special needs for children between the ages of 3 and 21. Michigan law goes further and specifies educational experiences to the age of 26. Contact your local school district's Department of Special Education.

You may want to work with a private educational specialist. This additional instruction combined with placing your child in the learning resource room at school may provide the teaching and skills needed by your youngster.

Leonard Kaplan

Resources

■ **Center for Human Development**
Beaumont Hospital, 3205 Coolidge Hwy., Royal Oak, MI 48072
(313) 288-2332, 8:00-4:00 M-F

■ **Eton Academy** provides individualized curriculum, especially designed for learning disabled students.
1775 Melton, Birmingham, MI 48008
(313) 642-1150, 8:30-2:20 M-F

▲ **Michigan Association for Children and Adults With Learning Disabilities** provides student advocacy, parent support, conferences and addresses of local chapters.
20777 Randall, Farmington Hills, MI 48024
☎ (313) 471-0790, 24 hour tape

▲ **Michigan Department of Education, Special Services** provides information for parents of Special Education students.
P.O. Box 30008, Lansing, MI 48909

■ **Michigan Dyslexia Institute** offers private tutoring
7125 Orchard Lake, Suite 209, West Bloomfield, MI 48322
(313) 737-0044

☎ **Project Find** of the Michigan State Board of Education Hotline. For early identification and resources call **1-800-252-0052**.

☎ **Learning Disabilities National Hotline,** sponsored by the National Association for Children with Learning Disabilities: **1-412-341-8077**

■ **Learning Disabilities:** *The Hidden Handicap* by John Merrow
(John Merrow Productions, $35.00) Audio cassette, 6 half-hour segments.
National Committee for Citizens in Education
10840 Little Patuxent Pkwy., Suite 301, Columbia, MD 21044
(301) 997-9300

❏ **Learning Disabilities:** *The Struggle from Adolescence toward Adulthood*
by William Cruickshank et al (Syracuse University Press, 1980, $12.95)

❏ **Learning Disabilities:** *A Family Affair* by Betty B. Osman
(Random House, 1979, $15.95)

❏ **The Magic Feather:** *The Truth About Special Education*
by Bill Granger (Dutton, 1986, $16.95)

❏ **The Misunderstood Child:** *A Guide for Learning Disabled Children*
by Larry B. Silver (McGraw-Hill, 1984, $14.95)

❏ **A National Directory of Four-Year Colleges', Two Year Colleges', and
Post- High Schools' Training Programs for Young People with
Learning Disabilities** by P.M. Fielding
(Partners in Publishing,1986, $17.95)
1419 W. First St., Tulsa OK 74127

❏ **Negotiating the Special Education Maze:** *A Guide for Parents and
Teachers* by W. Anderson, S. Chitwood and D. Hayden
(Prentice-Hall, 1982, $7.95)

❏ **No Easy Answers** by Sally Smith (Bantam, 1981, $4.95)

❏ **Reading, Writing and Rage** by Dorothey Ungerleide
(Jalmar Press, 1985, $12.95)

❏ **The Special Education Handbook:** *A Comprehensive Guide for Parents
and Educators* by Kenneth Shore
(Teachers College Press, Harper & Row, 1986, $14.95)

❏ **Turnabout Children:** *Overcoming Dyslexia and Other Learning Disabilities*
by M. MacCracken (Little, Brown, 1986, $16.95)

❏ **Your Child Can Win:** *Strategies, Activities and Games for Parents of
Children With Learning Disabilities* by Joan Noyes and Norma Mitchell
(Morrow, 1983, $11.95)

Q My daughter, 12, is really hepped up about math in sixth grade. How can I keep her enthusiasm up? I'm an engineer and I know I will need to buck a lot of people who will try to steer her elsewhere.

A In an increasingly technological age, it is more important than ever that all children understand and feel comfortable with mathematics. Too often girls are discouraged from actively pursuing math by their parents, teachers, counselors and peers. To insure that your daughter receives equitable treatment in both formal and informal math and science education, you can use the following strategies:

Encourage your daughter to take as many math classes in school as possible. If she finds math difficult, get her additional help, but don't let her drop out! Many professionals who use mathematics on a daily basis found math difficult in school.

Girls often think that it is unfeminine to like, or do well in, mathematics. Find some female role models in mathematics and science-based professions such as engineering, and have them talk to the students in your school and dispel this myth. Encourage these role models to not only discuss what their professional life is like but also how they combine family responsibilities with a career.

Make sure your daughter has science and mathematics-based toys, such as blocks, building sets, science kits and books, from preschool throughout childhood.

Discuss the importance of mathematics, from the practical, such as doing your income tax, to the professional.

Don't let your daughter be counseled into dropping a math course because "she won't need in later." The majority of college majors today require a full complement of high school math and science courses. A young girl does not know what she will need later in life. Encourage her to keep her options open.

Make sure that your daughter has access to and is at ease with computers. Check to see that your school's software is "girl friendly," that is, not "shoot-em up."

Encourage your daughter and her friends to participate in extracurricular science activities after school or at local science museums.

Our daughters will need mathematics. Don't let social barriers get in their way.

Cinda-Sue Davis

A The success of American science requires the full involvement of women. Unfortunately, female students as a group, continue to be considered incapable of, or uninterested in math. This stereotyping is reflected in the advice given by guidance counselors and parents. Peers also put pressure on their friends to avoid math. The disturbing results of this stereotyping can be seen in general aptitude tests taken at junior and senior years, and the decreasing participation by young women in science and math courses.

Solutions require a number of actions:

1. Any and all aspiring mathematicians and scientists require substantial parental support and encouragement. This is especially the case for girls.

2. Peer group support is available. Look to youth organizations such as scouts, church groups and school clubs.

3. There are numerous opportunities for expressions of ability and creativity in science fairs and science olympiads. Many of these group efforts allow special leadership and intellectual talents to be recognized.

4. As a parent you can stress and point out the everyday applications of mathematics. These range from simple tasks, such as evaluation of prices in stores, to more sophisticated efforts, such as the circuitry which runs computers, the telephones and cars.

5. It is important to take advantage of local non-traditional mathematics and science activities. Colleges and universities are constantly searching for good students and offer increasingly large numbers of enrichment opportunities on weekends and late hours on weekdays. Science museums conduct similar activities in a less formal environment which are both accessible and reassuring.

6. Math/science books are responding rapidly to the needs of girls and most no longer stereotype science as predominately male-oriented. Gift shops at science museums are excellent sources for books and home activities which promote development and inquiry into mathematics and science.

7. Above all, stress the pride and joy that comes with high achievement in whatever your daughter's area of interest might be. I believe this is the important ingredient in any career – the knowledge that your family fully supports you and shares in the excitement of your accomplishments.

Robert M. West

Resources

✔ **"Into the World of Today and Tomorrow" program,** co-sponsored by the Detroit Science Center and Metro Girl Scouts, provides activities to prepare young people for the scientific and technological challenges facing society today. (313) 577-8400.

✔ **Math Pentathlon,** a tournament of mathematics games is held annually in the spring. Contact Jane Schwarm, Frankenmuth, MI; (517) 652-9074. The Pentathlon Institute, Indianapolis, IN; (317) 782-1553

✔ **Women in Science Program,** University of Michigan. Cinda-Sue Davis, Ph.D., Director; 350 S. Thayer, Ann Arbor, MI 48104-1608; (313) 763-7225

✔ **"Yes, You Can"** program co-sponsored by Cranbrook Institute of Science and the Birmingham Branch of the American Association of University Women, encourages middle school girls to continue their studies of math and science. Workshops held annually in April. (313) 645-3230.

❑ *Growing Up Free: Raising Your Child in the '80's* by Letty C. Pogrebin (McGraw-Hill, $5.95)

❑ *How to Father a Successful Daughter* by Nicky Marone (McGraw-Hill, 1987, $16.95)

Q Our son goes to middle school this September. He doesn't seem mature enough or organized enough to "make it" in a school run so differently. How can we help at home to assure his smooth transition?

A Your child will be entering a new environment, but the children, as a group, will be introduced to school schedules and rules. Children usually need about a month to adapt to the new school and then they become very comfortable. If your district has not already done so, it would be helpful in mid-August to take your child to the new school, meet the principal and become familiar with the layout of building.

Within your family, encourage your son's maturity and ability to become more independent. Does he have responsibilities at home that must be done on a consistent basis? Is he responsible for the care of his clothing, cleaning up after a bath or coming home at a pre-designated time? Your establishment of rules, responsibilities and daily routines will help your son or daughter be self-sufficient and able to respond to a school schedule that requires responsibility. Summer is a good time to establish these rules if you have been lax in the past.

Another focus for your child's adjustment to a new middle school is to encourage lots of leisure reading and writing activities over the summer. Have your son visit the library once a month, meet the librarian and select books that will be of interest and help him to maintain the reading fluency and skills gained the past year in school. Watch for public television specials. Have your child watch them and then write a summary of the topics and ideas that were presented.

Reinforce these areas – routine responsibilities, independence and study skills – and your child will be prepared for a successful adjustment to middle school.

Janet Rosen

A The middle school is designed to meet the unique needs of this very important time in your son's life, when he will change from a child to a "middlescent." Brain development at this age allows the child to critically analyze and use information in new and different ways. He will, for the first time, be able to question everything that he has ever learned. The production of hormones during this time period will awaken new interests, often resulting in a desire for independence and a preoccupation with friendship groups. The middle school provides a wide variety of opportunities for questioning information, socializing appropriately, and developing independence.

Parents can help greatly by supporting their child and the school during these changes. If he is one of the early developers, help him accept and understand it, even if he does grow 6 inches in one year. If he is a late developer, assure him that it is normal for some boys of this age to still be less than 5 feet tall. Use the educators at the school as a resource and develop a partnership between the home and the school. By attending open houses, conferences and parent meetings, you can provide consistency for your son and demonstrate the importance you place on education. By checking on homework, monitoring grades and encouraging regular nightly study time, you will help him develop self-discipline. Finally, by encouraging him to participate in sports and social events at the school, you will further his ability to be well-rounded and well-liked.

Helene Mills

Resources

For parents:

❑ *Adolescent Development* by Lawrence Steinberg
  (Alfred A. Knof, 1984, $23.00)

❑ *All Grown Up and No Place to Go: Teenagers in Crisis* by David Elkind
  (Addison-Wesley, 1984, $8.95)

❑ *The Parents Guide to Teenagers* by L. H. Gross
(MacMillan, 1981, $14.95)

❑ *Suburban Youth in Cultural Crisis* by Ralph Larkin
(Oxford University Press, 1979, $2.50)

❑ *Why Am I So Miserable if These Are the Best Years of Life?*
by Eagan and Andrea Boroff (Avon, 1979, $2.50)

❑ *Your Child in School:* The Intermediate Years by Tom and Harriet Sobol
(Arbor House, 1987, $17.95)

For preteens

❑ *Growing and Changing:* A Handbook for Preteens
by Kathy McCoy and Charles Wibbelsman
(Perigree Books, 1986, $19.95)

✔ Also see resources under "Adolescence" in *Parenting and Family Life.*

Q Do we really need to be involved in our child's school? My husband and I both work outside the home and time is at a premium. Wouldn't the school just as soon we let them do *their* job: Educating our child?

A Parents do need to be involved. For much too long, many teachers have taken the position that parents should respond to the school when asked and, if not asked, keep away. The attitude that parents get in the way of learning was never appropriate and in today's world is even less appropriate.

Parents, whether they work outside the home or not, must insist on keeping involved in their children's education by participating as much as they can. Here are some things you can do:

Help your child with homework when possible.

Meet with the teacher frequently– even if there is nothing wrong.

Talk to your children about school and other activities and show your interest.

Gently, but sincerely, insist on quality from your child and from the school.

Demonstrate good habits to your child by getting involved yourself in some learning activity.

Read, read, read. Reading is the foundation for much learning. Be an example for your child. Demonstrate your involvement by reading books, magazines, newspapers.

Share ideas and thoughts with your children. A good discussion about ideas demonstrates that you are intellectually involved with things other than routine matters.

Participate in an activity with your youngster and follow it through to completion. For example, planting and caring for a garden together develops the concept of cooperation, a skill very important to success in school.

Keep your child informed regarding your communication with the school. Children will believe that "bad stuff" is taking place behind their backs if you are secretive or evasive. Youngsters must learn that communicating with teachers, principals and other professionsal is a positive, not negative activity.

Knowledge beats ignorance. Parents can be of tremendous help to the educational process by talking about teachers and schools in a positive manner. All of us have had some negative school experiences. Hopefully, the good outweighed the bad. Talk up the good.

Leonard Kaplan

Resources

▲ **Center for the Advancement of the Family**
Helps parents and educators develop skills in home-school relationships.
544 S. Rosedale, Grosse Pointe Woods, MI 48236
(313) 884-4652

▲ **Home and School Institute** offers the following books:

❑ *Families Learning Together.* A step-by-step program of simultaneous learning for adults and children. ($7.00 prepaid)

❑ *101 Activities for More Effective School-Community Involvement.* Suggestions to help schools put new life into community outreach programs. ($6.00 prepaid)

❑ *Three R's Plus.* Hundreds of home learning "recipes" for helping children from preschool through grade 8 with thinking, reading, writing, and math. ($7.00 prepaid)

✎ Home and School Institute, Special Projects Office
1201 16th St. N.W., Room 228, Washington, DC 20036
(202) 466-3633, 9-5 M-F

▲ **The National Committee for Citizens In Education** is a not-for-profit organization, dedicated to improving the quality of public education by being an advocate for home-school partnerships. They offer many publications and services including:

❑ *The Evidence Continues to Grow: Parent Involvement Improves Student Achievement – An Annotated Bibliography* by Anne Henderson (N.C.C.E.,1987, $10.00)

❑ *Beyond The Bake Sale: An Educator's Guide To Working With Parents* by Anne T. Henderson, Carl L. Marburger and Theodora Ooms (N.C.C.E., 1986, $14.95)

✎ National Committee for Citizens in Education
10840 Little Patuxent Pkwy., Suite 301, Columbia, MD 21044
(301) 997-9300, 8-4 M-F; recording after hours

☎ **ACCESS** is a free help line, sponsored by N.C.C.E., that provides parents with counseling and advises them of their rights regarding any problems with the home-school relationship.
1-800-NETWORK, 10-5 M-F

❑ *Mega Skills: How Families Can Help Children Succeed in School and Beyond* by Dorothy Rich (Houghton Mifflin, 1988, $8.95)

❑ *Parents As Partners: The Home and School Working Together* by Eugenia Hepworth Berger (Merrill Publishing Co., Toronto, 1988, $18.98)

✔ Your PTA can provide you with a variety of materials addressing specific issues concerning the home-school relationship, including:
The National PTA 88:Redbook Special Back to School Guide. (Free)
Michigan PTA 1011 N. Washington Ave., Lansing, MI 48906
(517) 485-4345

Q What rights do I, as a parent, have concerning my child's schooling? What are the laws regarding confidentiality of school records, attendance and other educational issues?

A The Family Education Rights and Privacy Act gives parents a number of rights. These include:

- access to a child's school records,
- the right to challenge content of school records,
- the right to be informed of rights under this act,
- the right to allow or prohibit the release of a child's records.

These are a parent's rights until the child turns 18. Remember that school employees sometimes share a child's records while performing educational duties.

Parents may require a child's absence from :

- sex education classes,
- classes discussing disease symptoms,
- silent meditation.

Schools must inform parents of these rights. Students do not need to participate in patriotic activities, such as singing the national anthem or reciting the Pledge of Allegiance.

Children are not required to attend public school:

- while attending confirmation classes during ages 12-13 (for up to 5 months),
- while attending regular religious classes for up to 2 hours a week,
- while employed by the state legislature as a page or messenger,
- if the child is under 9 years old and lives more than 2 1/2 miles from a school which provides no transportation,
- while regularly attending a state-approved non-public school.

Education is required until a child is 16.

Children have the right to public education regardless of mental or physical handicaps.

Parents may demand information about corporal punishment received by the child, including reasons and who was present during the punishment.

Federal and state law as well as administrative rules provide many safeguards for parents to assure a child's education, the confidentiality of records and appeal of educational decisions.

Most educational rights come from the state and federal constitutions, statutes and court decisions. However, elected local school boards have the right to set and establish policies and rights to meet local needs. The ballot box guarantees parents the right to influence school board policy to insure the best quality education.

Debbie Stabenow

Resources

■ **Parent Rights Card** listing 24 rights. (Item #NC9024PE, 25¢ each)
Also available in Spanish. (Item #NC9028PS, 25¢ each)

❑ *Parents, Schools and the Law* by David Schimmel and Louis Fischer (N.C.C.E., item #NC9042, 1987, $17.95)
Cards and book can be ordered from:
National Committee for Citizens in Education
10840 Little Patuxent Pkw., Suite 301, Columbia, MD 21044
(301) 997-9300

✔ Also see resources under "Parent Involvement."

Q I'm dreading my first parent-teacher conference. Please give me your best advice.

A Relax. You have a great deal of important information to share with the teacher, and the teacher, no doubt, will bring you up-to-date on your child's school performance. A successful parent-teacher conference provides the opportunity for mutual sharing. The teacher will welcome your insights into your child's strengths and areas of need as you perceive them.

You must be aware that, as the parent, you are – and will continue to be – the expert on what your children like to do, how they feel about school, what they dislike, what makes them anxious or fearful and how they respond to new situations.

Teachers often have a much better understanding of a child after a conference because the parent has given them information about the child that the teacher did not – and could not – know. Teachers, on the other hand, share with parents the child's abilities and skills in the school setting. They often will share information about the child's interaction with the other children. There may be times when the teacher and the parent both wonder if they are talking about the same child, for often a child behaves quite differently in school than at home.

If you have questions, do not hesitate to ask them. If you think you will not remember, jot them down before the conference.

The parent-teacher conference is an opportunity for two adults concerned about the same child, one objectively, the other subjectively, to share information and insights about the child in order to support or strengthen school performance and overall development. Remember you both have the same goal: to help your child get the most from his or her education.

Dorothy Kispert

A Parent-Teacher conferences should be a positive exchange between adults interested in facilitating the growth of youngsters. In addition to the regular conferences that are usually scheduled twice a year, parents and/or teachers may want to set up other meetings about specific problems or issues. Here's a list of "do's" to make these conferences more constructive:

1. Parents and teachers should communicate either by phone or by letter arranging the time, place and agenda for the meeting. None of the parties involved should be surprised in the conference.

2. Everyone's time is valuable. The conference should start and end on time.

3. When possible include the student in the conference. Translating to the student what went on can be confusing to your youngster. Having all interested parties together cuts down on this confusion.

4. If it is considered inappropriate to have the student present, at least inform the youngster about what is anticipated. The parent-teacher conference is not a plot between home and school to hurt children. Keeping the young person informed about the agenda and outcomes clears the air and eases anxiety.

5. Both teacher and parent should be prepared to offer suggestions on how each will assist the youngster and how they can work together. The conference should never be dominated by one side or another.

6. Remember parent-teacher conferences should be a regular series of events. Conferences held only at times of difficulty may be at the root of why many conferences are negative and quite frankly avoided by both home and school.

Let's lighten up, be positive and work *together*. After all, we all want to help kids. The youngster will be the beneficiary.

Leonard Kaplan

■ **Parent-Teacher Conferencing**
by Joseph C. Rotter and Edward H. Robinson (NEA, 1982, $2.50)
(Stock no. 1075-2-00) Order from:
Professional Library
National Education Association, P.O. Box 509 W. Haven, CT 06516

❏ **Getting the Most From the Public Schools**
by Sharon Clover (Pineapple Press, 1987, $15.95)

❏ **Help Your Child Make the Most of School**
by Terri Field (Kidsrights, $5.95)
1-800-892-KIDS

❏ **Parent, Teacher, Child:** Working Together in Children's Learning
by Dorothy Hamilton and Alex Griffiths (Methuen Inc., 1984, $8.50)

❏ **Parent-Teacher Conferencing**
by Gerda Lawrence and Madeline Hunter (NEA, 1978, $6.95)

❏ **Parent-Teacher Bond:** Relating, Responding, Rewarding
by Kevin J. Swick and Eleanor R. Duff. (Kendall-Hunt, 1978, $10.95)

✔ Also see resources under "Teacher-Student Relationships."

Q When we were kids we spent a lot of time outdoors, playing ball, skating, or just "running around." We also had gym every day at school. Our children, ages 6 and 8, only have physical education twice a week and spend a lot of time in front of the television. They're not overweight, but should I be concerned about their physical fitness?

A You certainly *should* be concerned. Recent studies show that 40 percent of American children between the ages of 5 and 8 already exhibit coronary risk factors such as high blood pressure, obesity and abnormally high levels of cholesterol. Fast-food diets are partly to blame, but too many kids are spending too many hours sitting in front of the tube.

"Children need to exercise at least 4 times a week," says Charles Kuntzleman, national program director of **Feelin' Good,** a kids' health program based in Spring Arbor, Mich.

The National PTA asked Kuntzleman to offer suggestions on how parents can encourage a desire for physical fitness in their children. He suggests the following:

Exercise yourself. Let your children see that keeping fit is an important part of life.

Run a family fitness check, and be sure to include yourself. Time a quick walk around the block, see how many push-ups you can do, bike, jog, dance – whatever works your heart and lungs. Then, after a month's efforts to improve your performance, check everybody again.

Design a chart that shows each family member's exercise plan and accomplishments; place it on the refrigerator or some other prominent place in the house.

Share a family fitness activity once a week, like walking, running, hiking or bicycling.

Equip your backyard with a swing set, rope or monkey bars so that physical activities are readily available to your kids.

If you don't have a backyard, scout out and use a nearby park or playground where your children can really let loose physically.

Limit TV and encourage more imaginative and beneficial pastimes, such as active play, sports teams or hobbies.

Help your children participate in fitness programs offered by your local Y or community center. Many bowling lanes, skating rinks and fitness clubs also offer programs for children.

Patricia Peart

Resources

✔ Check the library for Lerner Publications' "For Me" series which includes: *Bicycle Motocross Is For Me* by Tom Moran (1982); *Canoeing Is For Me* by Tom Moran, 1984; *Rock Climbing Is for Me* by Tom Hyden and Tim Anderson (1984).

❏ *Child Care: Parent Care* by Marilyn Heins and Anne M. Seiden (Doubleday, 1987, $17.95)

❏ *Healthy Kids for Life* by Charles Kuntzleman (Simon & Schuster, 1988, $16.95)

❏ *New Games for the Whole Family* by Dale N. LeFevre (Perigee Books, 1988, $9.95)

✔ Turn your TV into an excercise machine! There are work-out video tapes available for the whole family. Some examples (check your library or video store for others):
  ■ *Denise Austin's Family Workout* (Amway, $33.75) 1-800-544-7167
  ■ *Kids in Motion* (Young Hearts Records, $29.95) (213) 663-3223 (Can also be seen on Cable TV's Nickelodeon.)

Q My child is entering first grade. How can I help him as he begins to read?

A A child's attitude toward reading is crucial. It's important that reading be experienced as enjoyable. Here are some ways to foster a positive attitude toward reading:

Read to children even after they have begun to read. This exposes them to interesting and challenging material.

Choose books carefully. Have good and simple-to-read books available in your home

Follow your child's interests. Many children have gotten hooked on reading through joke and riddle books and simple books in areas that particularly interest them.

Talk to children about what you read in newspapers, books and magazines. Foster curiosity. If your child has questions, find the answers together in the encyclopedia.

Most libraries will issue cards to children. Let your child have his or her own library card and use it often.

Consider a family reading night once a week instead of television.

If your child wants to read to you, be encouraging, patient and interested. Learning to read takes time. If you put pressure on the child, he or she will experience reading as a chore rather than a joy.

If you suspect that your child is having serious difficulty with reading, talk to the child about what he or she finds difficult or doesn't like. You should also talk to the teacher about the difficulty and what steps are needed to further assess and remedy the situation.

Carol Mitchell

A Children who enjoy reading and being read to are children who will read. Unfortunately, some parents discourage kids' interest in reading because they concentrate so much on the minutiae – the alphabet, the letter sounds and the ability to pay rapt attention to stories – that they miss the warmth of the experience. Reading provides a wonderful excuse to snuggle or just to gaze at the pictures and dream.

Parents who enjoy reading typically have like-minded children. If your interest in reading is low, you may find that having a young child can be an incentive for you to read more. Here are some ways to help children discover the joys of reading:

Substitute reading for television, but don't act as if it's punishment.

Introduce children to libraries when they are young. To make trips pleasant, avoid the libraries' busy times, leave at the first sign of crankiness, and don't force your child to look at books.

When you read something you enjoy, share it with your child. Even preschoolers can relate to the sound of poetry or to a funny sentence from an article.

Avoid discouraging children from books that appear too difficult for them. If the story is too long for your child's attention span, summarize it or just talk about the pictures.

Don't disapprove of a child's interest in books written for younger kids. Even comic books can be incentive to reading.

Write "books" about your child. For example, toddlers may delight in a five-line story about their day. Older children may want to dictate stories while you write them down. Depending on the youngster's age, the tales may be disjointed or include details that are not appealing to adults. But try to refrain from editing so your youngsters can take full pleasure in hearing their creations.

Louise Reid Ritchie

Resources

■ *Becoming a Nation of Readers: What Parents Can Do*
by Marilyn R. Binkley (1988, 50¢)
What Parents Can Do, Consumer Information Center
Boulder, CO 81009-1188

❑ *Early Reading Through Experience* by E. Cromwell
(Acropolis, 1980, $9.95)

❑ *Eyeopeners! How to Choose and Use Children's Books About Real
People, Places, and Things* by Beverly Kobrin
(Penguin, 1988, $7.95)

❑ *Growing Up Reading* by Leonard Lamme (Scribner, 1986, $6.95)

❑ *On Learning to Read* by Bruno Bettelheim and Karen Zelan
(Vintage Books, 1982, $5.95)

❑ *R.I.F. (Reading Is Fundamental) Guide to Encouraging Young Readers*
by Ruth Graves (Doubleday, 1987, $8.95)

❑ *Taking Books to Heart* by Paul Copperman (Addison-Wesley, 1986, $9.95)

❑ *The Read-Aloud Handbook* by Jim Trelease
(Penguin Books, 1985, $7.95)

❑ *The Right Stuff to Teach your Children to Read* by James Hoffman
(School Zone Publishing Co., 1987, $12.95)
*ED NOTE: James Hoffman, Ed.D., is the Executive Vice President of
School Zone, a Michigan publishing company that has sold over 40 million
educational books and learning materials over the last 7 years. Their
beginning reading series, including* **Nine Men Chase a Hen** *and* **The Gum
on The Drum**, *are beautifully illustrated as well as interesting. (Available at
many retail outlets for approximately $2.00.)*
School Zone Publishing Company
1819 Industrial Drive, Grand Haven, MI 49417

✔ *When my children were growing up, I subscribed to* **The Horn Book**, *a
periodical with detailed reviews of children's literature. Ask for it at your
library or write to: The Horn Book, 31 St. James Avenue, Dept. HB,
Boston, MA 02116-4167. 1-800-325-1170. ($36.00 yr.)*

Alice R. McCarthy

Q Our son is repeating 5th grade. How can we make him feel OK about this?

A It is very important that you, as parents, find out why your child failed in school. Once you know, you can help him understand why and assure him he will receive whatever help he needs. Let him know that there is always a cause for academic failure; it may be intellectual, developmental or emotional.

Consider the possibilities of why learning is inhibited. Be sure you have tests for vision, hearing and other medical conditions that could be contributing to the problem. Attention deficit disorder is frequently missed. Subtle reading, writing, spelling and arithmetic deficits need to be considered.

There is help for children with learning deficiencies. Work closely with his school and his teacher. If the cause is emotional, work with a social worker, child guidance clinic, family service agency or private practitioners.

Do not make the child feel worse by scolding or demeaning him. Your child has strengths. Assure him of your support.

He may be teased by children. Don't deny this; he needs to talk about it. But most of all, reassure him that he is not "dumb" or "stupid."

Joseph Fischoff

Resources

❑ *Staying Back* by Janice Hale Hobby (Triad, 1982, $6.95)
Available from publisher (include $2.00 shipping):
Triad, 1110 N.W. 8th Ave., Gainsville, FL 32601

▲ **Michigan Association for Emotionally Disturbed Children**
(313) 356-2566, 8:30-4:30 M-F

✔ Also see resources under "Learning Disabilities." and "Report Cards."

Q Our son isn't doing very well in school. I've been in close touch with his teachers and I think I understand his learning problems. My husband isn't so understanding, however, and every report card results in a shouting match and humiliation for my son. What can I do?

A It is such a temptation for loving parents to overreact to poor grades, believing that, by insisting upon excellence, they will make their child successful in life. Your husband needs to understand that the child who is punished for poor grades – especially when there is a learning problem – will begin to see himself as unworthy and will have the tendency to give up, rather than trying to improve.

If you take the responsibility for grades, you are giving your son a tremendous amount of power and letting him off the hook. On the other hand, if your son is allowed to experience the consequences of poor grades, he will feel unsuccessful and unhappy. Then you can step in and help him become more successful. You become the good guy to a frustrated student.

Once you have become the "good guy," you are able to support the child with:

tutoring or help with homework,

providing positive feedback for successes,

a loving atmosphere,

any other help suggested by the teachers with whom you are collaborating.

I have seen a multitude of students reverse a destructive academic future through the support of parents and teachers working together. It takes a great deal of control and time on the part of the parent, but the rewards are worth it.

Helene Mills

A **Meet with a private learning specialist** who can explain your son's problems and set up a remedial program that will help your son to develop the skills to make him successful in school.

It is important that an in-depth diagnostic battery of tests be given. This battery of tests should include:

an intelligence test,

evaluation of skills in reading, mathematics and writing

evaluation of auditory memory, auditory discrimination, visual memory and visual perception skills.

Before any arrangements are made for this testing, make sure that you will receive a written report giving a complete interpretation of tests already administered, as well as recommendations to teaching staff working with your son.

It will be important for you and your husband to have a follow-up meeting with the learning specialist to answer any questions you might have after receiving the diagnostic test results. At this time the learning specialist can help your husband to understand the problem. A decision can be made if some family counseling might be appropriate to help your husband better understand his attitude toward your son's problems and learn how to cope with his feelings. The learning specialist may recommend in-school tutoring or outside tutoring for your son.

The combination of an in-depth evaluation, tutoring and possible family counseling should correct the problems you are experiencing.

Janet Rosen

Resources

- **"Helping Your Child Make the Grade "** by Sandy Dornbusch
  Can be ordered for 50¢ from:
  National School Public Relations Association
  1904 Association Drive, Reston, VA 22091

- ❏ *How to Help Your Child Succeed in School*
  by William and Susan Stainbeck (Meadowbrook, 1988, $5.95)

- ❏ *Improve your Grades: Effective Study and Test-Taking Techniques Not Taught in School* by Veltisezar B. Bautista
  (Bookhaus Publishers, 1988, $9.95)
  P.O. Box 299, East Detroit, MI 48021

- ❏ *Kids Who Underacheive: Strategies for Understanding and Parenting the Academically Troubled Child* by Lawrence J. Greene
  (Simon & Schuster, 1986, $7.95)

- ❏ *Smarter Kids* by Lawrence J. Greene (The Body Press, 1987, $16.95)

- ❏ *The Report Card Trap* by Beverly A. Haley (Betterway, 1985, $5.95)

How do you respond to your child's report card?

Researchers at Stanford University's Center for the Study of Families, Children and Youth have determined that the parent's response to a child's grades can have powerful influence on how well he or she performs the following term.

Director for the Center, Dr. Sanford Dornbusch, says that children who have parents who are extreme in either direction – strict or lenient – don't do as well as those whose parents are moderate, yet consistent.

Children with parents who are *inconsistent* do the worst. The best response is an "authoritative" one where parents expect mature behavior, establish clear standards and communicate openly.

What about monetary rewards? Dornbusch and his staff say praise and encouragement are fine, but not money. Paying a child for a good report card encourages an attitude that money is more important than learning.

Q How can I motivate my child to study? What kinds of study skills must he have in order to be successful at school?

A Motivating a child to study is often a concern of parents and teachers. One problem is that parents and teachers presume that the student is organized, can follow directions, take notes and study for tests.

Study skills should be taught and reviewed every year from fifth grade on. This should include how to take notes, outline, think critically, find main ideas and facts, and draw conclusions. Students also need to know how to write an essay and how to study for a multiple choice test versus an essay test.

To do well on SAT and ACT exams, the tests used by colleges as part of the admissions process, the middle school and high school curricula must have a program that is strong in developing vocabulary. The study of vocabulary lists, definitions and use of the newly defined words in writing must be a part of the student's learning.

Janet Rosen

A If you give your child the right foundation for home study in the early elementary years, the study habits he will need for the difficult junior high or middle school years will already be in place. Your foresight will help him cope with the increasing complexity and pressure of today's educational system.

Establish a short but regular time of the day to do something connected with school, even if he has no assigned homework After supper may be a good time because children need to play actively or go outdoors after the school day.

Create a consistent and quiet place in your home that is reserved for his study time. Be sure to provide good light, a comfortable temperature and adequate work space.

Never blend the homework space and time with television. Quiet background music is not distracting, but television is.

Use at least five minutes of the time to have your child read aloud to you.

Evelyn Petersen

✔ Also see resources under "Learning to Read," "Homework," and "Report Cards."

Q Many of my friends are having their young school-aged children tutored during the summer. Usually there is no particular academic problem. The tutoring is to push the children ahead academically or to "not lose what they have gained." I always thought kids needed a break. Isn't summer a time for play and fun?

A You are absolutely correct. Young children need a break in routine, a time when the pressure is off and they can play. They need time for social play with their friends, if they are to grow up as civilized people who care about each other.

At times tutoring is essential if a child is to keep up in school. But for the many children who are making normal progress or better, and are really trying hard to do well, being sent for tutoring can be a source of anxiety, a sign to children that their parents are not satisfied with them.

There has been a disturbing increase in parental pressure on children in recent years, particularly by many high achieving, middle-class parents. Recent research in suburban schools in southeast Michigan suggests grounds for concern. The increase in parental pressure for achievement has been accompanied by a serious increase in emotional problems, particularly depression, among young school-age children.

Eli Saltz

A Tutoring may be appropriate for a student who is falling behind or feeling a lack of intellectual self-esteem, but the average or above average child should be "taking a vacation" from traditional course work.

An "education" is what is left over when the facts are forgotten. It includes activities such as tennis lessons, swimming at the local "Y" or an art class. There is a great deal to be learned from family activities such as a visit to a museum, or Fort Wayne, a trip to Windsor over the bridge and back

---

through the tunnel, or a vacation planned around some historic event such as the Civil War. These experiences help your youngsters with their studies. The trips and activities give them something to write about in language arts class, and help them comprehend reading.

Their study in science and social science will become real because you have provided experiences which make lessons come alive. Summer activities reinforce learning and teach that learning can be fun.

Helene Mills

Resources

❑ *School's Out — Now What? Creative Choices for Your Child* by Joan M. Bergstrom (Ten Speed Press, 1984,$10.95)

❑ *The Hurried Child* by David Elkind (Addison-Wesley, 1981, $11.95)

❑ *The Too Precious Child* by Lynne Williams (Atheneum Press, 1987, $17.95)

Modern Museums

When someone suggests that you take your child to a museum, do you reply, "Oh, that's a nice idea," but say to yourself, "Borrrring!" ? If so, you probably haven't been to a museum lately. Many museums in Michigan are catering to kids with hands-on exhibits, special events, classes and activities throughout the summer (as well as afternoons and weekends during the school year).

Places like the Ann Arbor Hands-On Museum, the Jackson Space Center, Impressions Five in Lansing, the Flint and Detroit Children's Museums, Cranbrook Institute of Science , the Detroit Science Center, Greenfield Village and Henry Ford Museum, the Detroit Historical Museum, Historic Fort Wayne, the Afro-American Museum, and Your Heritage House (Detroit) offer fun, adventure and learning for all ages.

In addition to the larger, well-known museums, many communities have historic houses and interpretive farm and nature centers. (Be sure to call ahead, however, as these places are often staffed by volunteers and hours may be irregular.) Libraries, too, offer many summer programs.

Pat Peart

Q My child's teacher is totally insensitive to my daughter's abilities. How do I get the teacher to realize that my 8-year-old is a lot brighter than the teacher thinks she is?

A Frequently, parents see children one way and teachers another. That, of course, is due to the fact that you, as a parent, see your child in the home environment, reacting to all the kinds of things that go on with family members. You see the good and the bad. Teachers, on the other hand, see the youngster in a very different setting. They see the youngster in a classroom that is sometimes formal, totally created for organized learning, and often less conducive to an open and free expression.

Children reflect your values and attitudes. They bring to school your perceptions of what is important and what is not. Teachers bring to school their set of values regarding what is good and bad. Frequently, attitudes about learning held by the home and those values held by the school run into conflict because the teacher may represent a totally different view of what is important as compared to yours. As parents differ in their feelings of how children should be raised, teachers also differ in their attitudes toward kids and education.

We will never come to some agreement over what children should learn or how effective they are in the learning process if we do not come together to discuss, and agree upon, what is the right education for the individual child.

It is clear that you and the teacher have not spent nearly enough time trying to get to know each other, sharing views on not only your child, but children in general. My guess is that neither one of you is absolutely right or wrong, but each views the youngster from a different perspective.

The more we continue to sit in our respective houses or class-rooms making demands on children that do not take into consideration the attitudes of both home and school, the more children will be caught in the middle. Kids will attempt to do the impossible, that is to serve masters who are requiring different outcomes. Parents and teachers really need to sit down and talk about goals, rather than asking children to be a tennis ball in a match!

Leonard Kaplan

A **First, give the teacher a fair chance. Try to establish good communication.** If you are getting no where, consider whether you are accurate in your estimates of your child's ability and whether you are reasonable in your expectations of your child's teacher.

You may wish to have your child tested by an independent evaluator. If she turns out to be gifted, an enriched program is probably desirable. It may be unreasonable to expect a regular teacher to develop individualized programs. Contact your principal and request that the independent evaluation serve as the basis for placement in a gifted program. If there is no gifted program, investigate private schools, and talk to your child's principal and teacher about how you can supplement her school program.

If tests do not show your child to be gifted, consider whether your child is doing anything to turn off the teacher. Some bright children act inappropriately by answering all the questions, blurting out answers, finishing their work quickly and disrupting the class, challenging authority, etc. If your child is behaving this way, you need to help her act less impulsively. This could require outside professional help.

If your child is not doing anything to upset the teacher and classroom but is still not receiving fair treatment, be as assertive as necessary. Ask the principal to talk to the teacher or switch your child to another teacher. If you're still not satisfied, call the district's superintendent. Again, give the superintendent a fair shake. Tell him all you have tried to do to use the proper channels and improve the situation.

Arthur Robin

Q At a recent parent-teacher conference my 7-year-old daughter's teacher spent half of the 15-minute conference telling me my daughter is conceited and self-centered. I sat stunned listening and finally asked how she was doing academically. The reply was, "She is tops in phonics, math and reading and is doing well in everything else. She listens, doesn't talk back, is popular and has lots of friends." I feel everyone has a right to feel good about themselves. Can children be conceited at such a young age? Should we meet with the teacher or the teacher and the principal? We don't want to make it worse for our daughter. The teacher may dislike our daughter even more if we confront her.

A Whoever said that parenting is easy, lied. Try not to overreact. Taking this situation out of context and building it into a monumental event does neither you nor your daughter any good. Your description of your child leaves the impression that she's a pretty neat kid, happy, doing well, popular, doing all the things we would hope and expect. I know a lot of parents who would love a copy of your daughter and be very happy.

Your reaction to the teacher should not spill over to your child. If your child begins to believe that you have reservations about the competence of her teacher, she, too, will begin to question not only her teacher's competence, but also the role of an educator as a positive influence. We have too many children who come to school with very negative attitudes about what education is and can be for them that were instilled by negative parents.

Egocentrism is a natural characteristic of children. It is neither harmful nor destructive. It does not normally lead to poorly functioning adults or egomaniacs. The Swiss psychologist, Jean Piaget, clearly points out that egocentrism helps us develop positive self-esteem. As parents and teachers we help youngsters begin to understand that the personal pronouns, I and me, eventually must include we and us. I hope that the teacher understands that all children possess egocentric characteristics and either has forgotten this or possibly needs to reacquaint herself with some of the developmental characteristics of children.

With as much tact and humor as possible, go back and visit the teacher with more of a chat in mind than a confrontation. As the two of you get to know one another better, issues can be resolved. I'm also sure that you will have a sympathetic ear from your child's principal. Invite him to join your next conference. Above all, do not permit your daughter to become a tennis ball in a match between home and school. That serves no purpose.

Leonard Kaplan

| A | **Study after study demonstrates the importance of good self-esteem.** After satisfying the basic needs of security and substance, the most pressing problem of a human being is to feel good about himself. Our core self-concept is determined mainly by others, by how they relate and give feedback. If children get positive, specific feedback about their looks and behavior, they will begin to perceive themselves as good. If they receive negative feedback, they will continue to be preoccupied with themselves. This preoccupation causes a delay in the developmental process, including the ability to learn and the desire to help others. If you would like to read further on this subject, I suggest Abraham Maslow's *The Farthest Reaches of Human Nature* (Peter Smith Publisher, $14.25).

You and your family have obviously done a great job of giving positive feedback to your daughter, for she sounds like she has a good self-concept.

Let's take a look at the misunderstandings related to the self-esteem. **First, vanity is caused by a preoccupation with appearances.** Someone who is vain has had too much emphasis placed upon beauty or clothing, etc., and not enough importance on learning, relationships, or their developing personality. These individuals are so self-preoccupied they are not able to care about getting an education, developing relationships with others, or helping others to grow. Your child certainly does not fit this description. **Second, conceit is a preoccupation with self and is the result of a poor self-concept.** It is a defense for not feeling good about ourselves. The child gets "stuck" at this level of development and continues to seek the esteem of others. These children do not do well in school and seldom have healthy, positive relationships with other children. Your daughter's behavior, concern for others, accomplishments in school, and cooperation at home seem to contradict this description.

What should you do about all this? First, don't let it interfere with your good relationship with her. She sounds like a normal, healthy, adorable young lady and she needs you to continue to show her love, affection, and to give positive responses. Second, you and your husband need to have another talk with the teacher about your daughter's behavior. Parents and teachers have the same goals for kids and should be partners in the process of reaching those goals. Share this column to help clarify some of the misunderstandings the teacher may have about self-esteem. Ask clarifying questions to determine whether your daughter is held up on her development in any way that is not apparent in your letter. Teachers see another side of a child and it is important that parents know what takes place at school, so they can respond to it better at home.

Helene Mills

☎ **(1-800-NETWORK)** Toll-Free Help Line
Advises parents who call with school-related problems.

❏ *Parent, Teacher, Child: Working Together in Children's Learning*
by Dorothy Hamilton and Alex Griffiths (Metheun Inc., 1984, $8.50)

❏ *Teachers and Parents:* An Adult-to-Adult Approach
by Dorothy Rich (Stock No 0277-6-00, $9.95)
National Education Association Professional Library
P.O. Box 509, Westhaven, CT 96516, (203) 934-2669, 9-4:30, M-F
*ED NOTE: There are strengths in every family that can be mobilized into
effective educational action. Teachers and parents complement each other
to help children achieve.*

✔ Also see resources under "Parent Involvement" and "Parent-Teacher
Conferences."

10 Things That Teachers Wish Parents Would Do

❶ Provide the resources at home for reading and learning.

❷ Set a good example.

❸ Encourage children to try to do their best in school.

❹ Emphasize academics.

❺ Support the school's rules and goals.

❻ Use pressure positively.

❼ Call teachers more often and earlier if there is a problem.

❽ Take responsibility as parents.

❾ View drinking alcoholic beverages by underage youth and excessive
partying as a serious matter, not a joke.

❿ Be aware of what is going on in the school and become more involved
in school activities.

The National PTA

Q What standard tests are currently being administered in public schools and how are test results used?

A Standardized testing is only one method of many approaches used to appraise student growth and development. These tests tell us how students have progressed in relation to the norm group, and provide an estimate of the effectiveness of the schools. Objective test information, along with a student's daily classroom performance, can provide the basis for parent/teacher conferences and home/school cooperation.

A good testing program closely aligns test materials and the testing purpose. Test scores may be used for curriculum development, curriculum revision, remedial work with individual students, predictions of further accomplishments and reports to parents, administrators, Boards of Education and the community.

Michigan has developed its own **Michigan Educational Assessment Program (MEAP)** test, an objective-referenced test, administered at the 4th, 7th and 10th grade levels for all Michigan public shcool students. Its purpose is to determine attainment of the State's essential performance objectives for reading and math. Starting in Fall 1989, students at grades 5, 8 and 11 will be tested in science. Additionally, a writing test will be piloted in 36 selected schools for potential implementation in grades 3, 6 and 9 during Spring 1989.

In addition to MEAP, tests in these categories are likely to be given:

Achievement Tests are composed of separate tests in the different skill areas. At the elementary and junior high levels these generally include tests in reading, language, arithmetic and study skills. Examples are **California Achievement Tests, Comprehensive Tests of Basic Skills, Iowa Tests of Basic Skills, Metropolitan Achievement Tests and Stan-**

ford Achievement Tests. Such batteries are helpful for broadening teacher understanding of pupils and for instructional planning. At the secondary level, the achievement batteries also assess the generalized outcomes of instruction.

Reading Tests seek to identify individual strengths and weaknesses. Examples are the **Prescriptive Reading Inventory** at the elementary level and **Gates-MacGinite Reading Tests** and the **Stanford Diagnostic Reading Test** at the elementary/secondary levels.

Aptitude Tests are designed to measure capacities in various ability areas that are related to later educational and vocational success. Examples are the **Differential Aptitude Tests (DAT), Preliminary Scholastic Aptitude Test (PSAT), Scholastic Aptitude Test (SAT)** and the **American College Test (ACT).**

Specialized Testing may be administered to determine a student's qualifications and potential placement in a variety of special education opportunities. The **Gesell Test** to identify children eligible for the *Early Fives* program is often given. Mental ability tests are sometimes used to determine IQ information about pupils' differential capacities.

Evaluation in education should be a continuous process of gathering and weighing information that indicates changes in the behavior of students as they progress through school. My school district, Bedford Public Schools, has a comprehensive testing program typical of many school districts.

Our K-12 scope appears on the following pages.

Herbert Moyer

Grade	Name of Test	Purpose
Pre-K	Gesell	Identify children eligible for *Young Fives* Kindergarten.
K	Metropolitan Readiness	Aid decisions regarding admissions to 1st grade by predicting success in beginning reading and mathematics.
1-6	Gates-MacGinite Reading	Assist in placement in reading groups. Identify progress in vocabu- and comprehension.
3, 6	Stanford Achievement	Survey achievements in basic skills. Help the child and parents understand the child's strengths and weaknesses. Diagnose strengths and weaknesses in group and individual performance. Evaluate curricular programming.
4, 7, 10	Michigan Educational Assessment Program	Determine attainment of State's essential perfor- mance objectives in read- ing and mathemetics.
8	Orleans-Hanna	Use in tandem with teacher recommendation to predict success in Algebra I.

Grade	Name of Test	Purpose
9	Differential Aptitude Test	Study student abilities in eight aptitude areas. Use DAT profile as a basis for early vocational counseling and course selection.
10	Preliminary American College Test (P-ACT)	Assess aptitude for college level academic work
10/11	Preliminary Scholastic Aptitude Test (PSAT)	Use as preliminary estimate of aptitude for college level academic work.
11/12	American College Test (ACT)	Assess aptitude for college level academic work.
12	Scholastic Aptitude Test (SAT)	Assess aptitude for college level academic work.
12	Armed Service Vocational Aptitude Battery	Help students make appropriate career decisions.
12	Stanford Test of Academic Skills (Task 2)	Diagnose strengths and weaknesses in group performance. Determine exit skills of seniors. Evaluate curricular programming.

Parenting and Family Life

Q There are days when my teen-age son and I will argue for hours about something and never resolve it. Please give me some pointers on how to avoid arguments and ways to communicate more positively.

A Teens are experts at drawing parents into arguments. It is vital that *you* decide what is negotiable and what is not. If the matter is not negotiable, tell your child that you welcome his opinion and conversation on many topics, but that particular matter (going to a rock concert or getting a car, perhaps) is not open for discussion. State your position briefly. It's not necessary to argue or defend it.

To help your teen "save face" and feel less discounted in matters that you control, you can let him have "the last word." First tell him that you are not going to change your mind. Then ask, "Do you have anything else to say?" Whatever he says, just let it stand! Nothing else need be said; discussion closed. The teen will feel better because he has had a chance to say something, but you remain in control.

Here are a few tips on keeping communication consistently positive. Your attitude (you are always willing to talk and to listen) is the message your son will hear loud and clear, despite any rough spots in communication.

1. Use questions sparingly. Resist the urge to know everything your child is thinking or planning.

2. Try not to be defensive. Ignore some of the careless, general criticisms that teens make.

3. Offer your advice or feedback even if it seems unwelcome, but don't keep repeating it. (They do hear you the first time.)

4. Talk about yourself instead of the teen, your own fears and feelings or memories of when you were a teen.

5. Be accessible. Teens often blurt things out or want to talk at strange times. Don't overreact. Just be ready to listen anytime, anywhere.

Evelyn Petersen

Resources

✎ **"Successful Parenting"** by Elaine Wasserman (79¢ + 50¢ postage) Includes ways to improve parent-child communication.
Minerva Press Inc.
6653 Andersonville Road, Waterford, MI 48095

❏ *Teen Is a Four Letter Word: A Survival Kit for Parents*
by Joan W. Anderson (Better Way Publications, 1983, $5.95)

For Teens:

❏ *How to Live with Parents & Teachers* by Eric W. Johnson
(Westminster Press, 1986, $9.95)

❏ Also see resources under other "Adolescence" questions.

Q I'd like to get together with other parents to set guidelines for our children regarding curfews, and parties with alcohol and drugs. Any suggestions?

A Parents of children who are socializing together should be encouraged to call each other in advance to verify beginning and ending times of an event, the presence of an adult, and that alcohol won't be served.

One technique for setting community-wide standards is to establish a **"safe homes"** program. Parents who join agree not to allow alcohol to be served to under-age young people at social occasions in their home or on their property. They also are encouraged to establish definite party hours, limit guest lists, not allow guests who leave to return and not let guests who have been drinking drive home.

They should call the parents of anyone caught drinking – or call the police if necessary – and develop agreed-upon procedures for dealing with problems such as party crashers. The list of "safe homes" should be distributed to parents in the community. Parents can also display their membership pledge at home for children and guests to see. Standards for curfews should be reasonable and appropriate for the age of the child.

Ilona Milke

Resources

📚*Michigan Parent Group Handbook: Preventing Teenage Drinking and Other Drug Problems* (Free)
Substance Abuse and Traffic Information Center
925 E. Kalamazoo St., Lansing, MI 48912

▲ **Michigan Communities in Action for Drug-Free Youth** (MCADY)
State-wide volunteer network and resource center. Ideas, research data, and annual adult/youth conference. Helps parents and youths form support groups. Also sponsors **REACH,** a youth (age 14-19) project of the National Federation of Parents, encouraging youth to "be a part of the solution" to alcohol and drug problems.
470 N. Woodward, Birmingham, MI 48009
(313) 642-6270 or 1-800-622-6849

▲ **Safe Homes**
National Headquarters, P.O. Box 216, Mahwah, NJ 07430
(201) 529-3330
> For good examples of local programs contact:
> **Birmingham-Bloomfield Families in Action**
> P.O. Box 1088, Birmingham, MI 48012
> (313) 644-2245
> **Substance Abuse Community Council of Grosse Pointe** (SAC2)
> Send $1.00. for "As Parents We Will."
> P.O. Box 36150, Grosse Pointe Farms, MI 48236

✔ Aid Association for Lutherns has available for loan, through AAL branches in Michigan, an excellent film, *Drug-Free Kids*, with a study guide. Additional materials are available through the Wisconsin office.
4321 N. Ballard Rd., Appleton, WI 54919
(414) 734-5721

❏ *Setting Limits: Parents, Kids and Drugs* by William La Fountain (Hazelden, 1982, $1.75)

Q My children, 11 and 14, seem to be drawing away from our family. They are beginning to live in a world quite apart from us in spite of our all being in one house. Their music, friends, sports are all different from ours. Should we worry about peer pressure?

A Fitting into the gang – or peer group – becomes increasingly important to children between the ages of 8 and 12. Research indicates this is particularly true for girls who are generally more interested than boys in seeking social approval. However, both boys and girls in this age group become significantly more alert to the way "the group" thinks, acts, dresses and talks. This is the age of secret codes and language not meant for adults, dressing and looking alike, rituals, clubs and conforming to a set of values promoted by the group.

Children need to spend time with their peers and have a certain amount of privacy. This enables them to develop a sense of solidarity outside the family, which they will need for effective social functioning and independence in the future. It also gives them opportunities to explore a variety of ideas outside the immediate culture of their own families.

Not to conform to peer-group values means possibly not belonging, and popularity can often depend on how closely a child adheres to a particular group's values. When values promoted by the group (for example, stealing to get into the group) conflict with those held by the child's family, a child may experience considerable stress. Not surprisingly, children who spend most of their leisure time with peers – and very little with their parents – will feel more compelled to go with group values. Those children who are at least equally involved with parents, and who feel supported and valued by their parents, will lean toward parental values –

even in the face of strong opinions held by the all-cherished group.

While the peer group is an important and necessary socializing factor in every child's life, parents often worry that children will be overly influenced by peers and possibly in negative directions. They can buffer that fear by making sure there is a balance between peer group and family involvement in their child's social life. This requires not just "quality" time spent with the child but also a certain quantity of positive interaction time as the child moves toward adolescence.

Anne Soderman

A During the teen years, young people tend to pull away from the family in order to define themselves as individuals and establish their own sense of identity – including personal values and morals, relationships and career direction. Teens often turn to their peer group for a sense of belonging outside of the family. Their friends then can have much influence over how they are going to behave. Adolescents will succumb to peer pressure because they are searching for some direction and guidance in understanding themselves or feeling as if they belong to a group.

Parents can lessen the impact of peer pressure in several ways.

First of all, don't take it personally if your teen is pulling away from you and turning to friends. This is a natural part of the adolescent years. You are still needed as parents even if it seems like your child is rejecting you.

Provide an atmosphere where teens can express their viewpoints openly. Start discussions at the dinner table about sexual involvement, drugs and alcohol, etc. Let your teen know that these topics are not restricted to talks with their friends. If you make it known that you are open to discussing any issue, your teen will be more likely to seek out your opinion. This openness also makes it more likely that your child will choose friends who support your value system.

Help your teen go through the steps of personal decision-making. Teens need to know that you respect their ability to make decisions and to be responsible so that they can develop some confidence in themselves. They are more likely to resist peer pressure if they have a sense of their own identity, feel self-confident and know that they have your support.

Katherine Mills

A **You want to encourage your child to expand his or her world view beyond the boundaries of home during the teenage years.** It is a time when children are confronted with other people's lifestyles and values which my be in conflict with their own.

Effective communication is based on mutual understanding. The more you know about your child's world, the easier it is to relate.

Involve yourself in your child's school life. Attend conferences and other school activities. You can't teach your child to be street smart if you don't know what's happening in the street.

Learn your children's language as a means to understanding their world. Understand the functions of their fads, hairstyles, music, etc. It is not necessary to fully appreciate or accept them. Don't be overly critical.

Get to know their friends. Encourage them to bring friends home.

Help your child develop a strong sense of self. If they know who they are and what they want to be, it will be easier for them to make good decisions.

Donald Davis

❏ **Helping Your Child Handle Stress** by Katherine Kersey
(Acropolis, 1985, $8.95)

❏ **How to Deal With Your Acting-Up Teenager:** *Practical Help For Desperate Parents* by the Bayards. (M. Evans, 1983, $8.95)

❏ **How to Survive Your Adolescents' Adolescence**
by Robert Kolodny, Nancy J. Kolodny, Thomas Brattner and Cheryl Deep
(Little Brown, 1986, $9.95)

❏ **Raising Each Other:** *A Book for Parents and Teens*
by Jeanne Brondino *et al* (Hunter House, 1987, $7.95)
The writings of 50 high school students who discuss freedom, privacy,
trust, drugs, sex, religion and family values.

❏ **Raising Children For Success** by Stephen Glenn with Jane Nelsen
(Sunrise Press, 1987, $7.95)
4984 Arboleda Dr., Fair Oaks, CA

❏ **The Quicksilver Years:** *The Hopes and Fears of Early Adolescence*
by Peter Benson et al (Harper & Row, 1987, $13.95)

Q Our 12-year-old son daydreams and often seems withdrawn and unhappy. He is the middle child between two sisters. He is nice looking, although he has a dark mole on his cheek. Could birth order and physical appearance affect the way my son feels about himself?

A The biological events of puberty and its effects on body image, moods and relationships are unavoidable and a necessary part of growing up. It is often at this time that developing positive self-esteem becomes a major problem for youngsters.

While there are conflicting opinions about the role of birth order and an adolescent's conception of himself, the role of one's physical appearance has been well established. There is a difference between girls and boys at this age. At the time of puberty, girls may have a decline in good feelings about themselves. With boys, an early maturing seems to have a positive effect on self-esteem.

At the age of 12 it is not unusual that conflict in family discussions begins to increase, with boys usually becoming more dominant in these conversations with parents. The many other factors that might affect a young boy at the age of 12 include the change from elementary to junior high school or middle school with the different system of attending classes.

Puberty is a time when parents must be even more sensitive than in other periods to the needs of the growing young adolescent. Have you asked your son about the mole on his cheek? And, if indeed he doesn't want it there, have you consulted with a dermatologist about the possibility about having it removed?

Charles C. Vincent

A Physical appearance can certainly affect the way one feels about oneself. Although you said that you think your son is nice looking, has he ever mentioned to you that he thinks he is unattractive? If he is terribly bothered by the mole on his face, you may want to see a plastic surgeon for consultation. His birth order position is probably playing a minor role in producing his unhappiness, but look more closely at how his sisters treat him. Do they tease or humiliate him? Do they dominate him? Do they allow him input into their plans?

Have a private talk with your son, sharing your observations that he appears sad and withdrawn. Ask him if there is anything anyone in the family could do to change, which would be helpful to him. Try to ask open-ended questions which will allow him the greatest opportunity to share his thoughts. Don't be too quick to jump in and give your advice. Listen to his feelings – without being judgmental and critical.

Set up an appointment with your son's school counselor. Check out his counselor's observations of your son. How has his school performance been? Try to determine if he is under too much pressure at school. What do his standardized test scores say about his performance? Have his grades slipped recently? What extracurricular activities does he enjoy? Capitalize on his strengths. Help him develop interests in activities in which he can achieve success.

If you feel his sadness and daydreaming are excessive, you should consider contacting the **Psychologist Referral Service at (313) 642-2508** for the name of a licensed psychologist. You may also want to discuss your son's problems with your family doctor or pediatrician. A professional evaluation may be reassuring and help steer you in the right direction.

Steven Spector

<hr>

Resources

❑ *Coping With Teenage Depression* by K. McCoy
   (New American Library, 1983, $7.95.

✔ Also see resources under other "Adolescence" questions.

Q I know my kids are watching too much TV. I've tried to cut back but they always say they're bored and start fighting. The only time we have peace in this house is when we are all watching TV. What can I do?

A Most experts disagree on the right amount of TV viewing for children. Concerned parents agree that their children watch too much TV. Rather than give up TV completely, I suggest reducing the viewing time. One way to do this is to introduce the *TOT* (**Turn Off TV**) hour. TOT gives families a chance to function as a team and to get to know each other. One mother who tried the TOT said she never realized that conversations with her children consisted of telling them what to do, and asking questions. At her children's request they added more TOT hours, found they were no longer TV addicts and were enjoying family life more. TOT families become stronger and start to relate as real people. Here are a few activities families can do related to TV:

Make your own quiz programs using the same format as your favorite TV quiz program. I use my son's social science book. It makes studying a pleasure.

Play charades, using TV characters in the role they play on TV or a different role. These games help develop awareness of characterization.

Use TV as a guide to picking out a book that will appeal to your whole family. Get a "classic" like *Peter Pan, Frankenstein* or *Winnie the Pooh*. It's fun to compare the original with the Hollywood treatment.

Make a commercial. By selling an item in 30 seconds children can learn why commercials are constructed as they are.

Involve everyone in making family meals. Children enjoy cooking from scratch. Our young TV generation is convinced that everything is either frozen or comes from a box. Talk about the effects TV has on your eating habits.

Children barely remember what episode they watched on TV last week, yet they can remember what they did with their families for a lifetime.

Marilyn Droz

A **Finding alternatives for television viewing has tremendous payoffs in the intellectual, social and emotional development of the child as well as the health of the family unit.** During the years that our children were young and until they reached senior high school, every Friday evening and Sunday were reserved for the family.

Sundays included visiting relatives and/or going places together such as the zoo, Greenfield Village, Cranbrook, the Detroit Science Center, a park or a museum. Friday was called "Family Night" and was an organized time to play together. Sometimes we played games such as Monopoly or Fish. Sometimes we read an ongoing story out loud. We especially enjoyed Tom Sawyer because we liked to take turns trying the dialect.

Our favorite project lasted about two years of Fridays. Each Friday evening we would pretend that we were visiting another country or culture. We prepared for the evening all week long by learning about the customs of that place and preparing the appropriate food, outfits and entertainment. When we "visited" Mexico, we played with a piñata, wore colorful clothing and ate tamales and tacos. When we "visited" Hawaii, we had a luau, complete with grass skirts, and learned some of the hand motions of the hula dancers. When we "visited" Japan, we ate around the coffee table, used chopsticks and played oriental games. All of the time and effort necessary to complete these projects and outings was worth it in memories as well as for family and personal development.

Your family can think of just as many imaginative ways to lick the blahs of TV viewing.

Helene Mills

Resources

▲ **Council for Children's Television and the Media**
offers brochures on "Viewing Tips," "Gently Reduce TV Time," "TOT Hour"
and "Alternatives to TV."
33290 W. Fourteen Mile Rd., West Bloomfield, MI 48322
(313) 489-5499

❑ *After You Turn Off the TV Set: Fresh Ideas for Enjoying Family Time*
by Frances Moore Lappe (Ballantine Press, 1985, $7.95)

❑ *How to Play With Your Children* by Brian Sutton-Smith
(Dutton, 1974, $6.95)

✔ *There are a number of "activity books" which feature projects,
experiments, cooking and crafts for children. Check your library or
bookstore shelves.*

✔ *Board games were a favorite form of family entertainment long before the
dawning of video. And despite the competition from the tube, there are
more – and better – games available now than ever before. Quite a few
award-winning games have been invented and manufactured in Michigan:*

■ **Alex's Fun and Learning Games** offer *The Teddy Bear Factory Game*
for preschoolers and *The Silly Game* for older children.
P.O. Box 810, Birmingham, MI 48012; (313) 642-0243

■ **Aristoplay Ltd.** offers award winners such as *Artdeck, By Jove,
Dinosaurs and Things, Music Maestro,* and *Paleopals.* All are
beautifully done, fun as well as educational, and designed to be played
at different skill levels.
Available at speciality, book and toy stores or directly from:
P.O. Box 7645, Ann Arbor, MI 48107; (313) 995-4353

■ **Michigan PTA** offers *American Trivia Challenge-Michigan Style*
available through local PTA units or:
Michigan PTA, 1011 N. Washington Ave., Lansing, MI 48096
(517) 485-4345

■ **Musical Attractions** is a board game for children, parents and
grandparents, using titles of popular music from 1900-1986.
Available at specialty stores or directly from:
Hovis & MacLennan, P.O. Box 1184, Dearborn, MI 48121
(313) 336-8782

Q Our grandson, 12, is lying and stealing from family members. Recently he took a check to the bank with a note forged on the back asking the bank to cash the check. He seems obsessed with money. We are very worried and embarrassed about his behavior and know we must help him. How?

A Stealing money from the family and lying about it, along with check forgery, represents a very serious behavioral emotional difficulty in need of immediate intervention. All teenagers occasionally think about taking money but most have the impulse control to think through the consequences and avoid such an anti-social action. The fact that your grandson has not been able to communicate his needs or wants to his family in a more appropriate way than stealing suggests that there has been a major breakdown in parent-child relations. I would question whether he has internalized appropriate moral values. He may be unduly influenced by anti-social friends.

His family needs to take strong, immediate action. I suggest they:

Clearly communicate to him that stealing is illegal, immoral and unacceptable and establish clear negative consequences for any further episodes of stealing.

Contact their local police station and arrange to have a police officer have a talk with your grandson about the legal aspects of stealing. A tour of the jail or youth home together with a strongly worded discussion coming from a helpful police officer may make an impression.

Establish a careful monitoring system to know where he is at all times and enforce it vigorously.

Take your grandson to a qualified mental health professional for an evaluation and immediate therapy. The stealing could be a symptom of a variety of behavior disorders and only a further evaluation could shed light on this.

Arthur Robin

A **Lying and stealing can be a common childhood problem.** In determining how serious the problem is, you need to know what led up to the behavior and what the consequences were for the child. Stealing can be a result of peer pressure or a source of funds for buying friendship, drugs or alcohol. Some children steal in reaction to family problems as a cry for help or as a plea that someone notice them. Sometimes stealing is simply an experiment or impulse which, with the appropriate consequence, is not repeated.

When stealing occurs, it is important to discuss calmly with the child what led up to it. If it was simply an impulse, a logical consequence, such as returning what was stolen – with an apology, is generally effective. If the stealing is part of a more complex problem, such as peer pressure, drugs or family stress, these problems must be solved or the stealing will likely continue. For example: If a child's stealing enhances his position in his peer group, this consequence may outweigh any consequence or punishment the parent enforces.

Family counseling is often most helpful in solving these more complex problems. A number of social service agencies and community mental health centers offer these services to families. Local psychological, social worker and psychiatric associations can refer you to private practitioners who specialize in families.

Carol Mitchell

✔ *To find a counseling service, call your local Social Service Department (listed in the White Pages under Michigan, State of). Also contact your local crisis center, your principal, United Way or United Community Services for a referral.*

✔ *Also see resources under "Responsibility."*

Q My son, 5, often seems angry and says "no" far more than "yes." Recently, at the barber shop, he screamed and started to kick and hit me – *and the barber!* What's wrong? How can I help him?

A Anger is a symptom. Look for the message behind the behavior. Talk to him. By the age of 5, children should be encouraged to express their feelings in words so that you both know exactly what is bothering them. Acknowledge his feelings with statements such as, "I know you don't like getting your hair cut, but we have to do this. If you sit quietly it won't take long." Compliment him on any good behavior. Avoid taking him places he really dislikes when he is tired and hungry. This will add to his frustration and irritability. If possible, allow him to bring a toy or a book to make this unpleasant chore a little more tolerable. Saying "no" is a very normal way that young children express their growing independence from you. This is a positive sign. It does not have to represent hostility or unhappiness.

K. Noelle Clark

A Hitting and kicking others should never be accepted and discipline should follow immediately. Even if he has been reared in a permissive manner, you need to make it clear that there are limits to what adults will tolerate. If he does not respect the limits, he should be disciplined.

On the other hand, he may be afraid and expressing anger with words and actions to avoid feeling fear. Has anything happened that could make him afraid? Are there changes at home such as the birth of a baby, a family move, or fighting in your family?

Two approaches have been successful and can be used together at times. He can be told that if he is well-behaved, he can chose an activity, at the end of the day, that he likes to do. This should be repeated day after day.

The other approach is to tell him grown-ups talk to each other. Although he is angry, he also may be worried or frightened. But since he is quite grown up at 5, he can talk with you about it and you can help him.

Do not pay attention every time he says "no." If he does what you want, do not remind him he said "no." If you do, his behavior will be reinforced.

Joseph Fischoff

Resources

❑ *Behavior Management: You Can't Make Me* by Judith K. Schneider (C.A.P.E., 1987, $6.95) Home/Study Program also available. C.A.P.E. Center, 5924 Royal Lane, Suite 216, Dallas, TX 75230

❑ *Mister Rogers' How Families Grow* by Fred Rogers and Barry Head (Berkley Books, 1988, $7.95)

❑ *Loving Your Child Is Not Enough: Positive Discipline That Works* by Nancy Samalin and Martha Jablow (Viking, 1987, $15.95)

❑ *Positive Discipline: Teaching Children Self-Discipline, Responsibility, Cooperation and Problem-Solving Skills* by Jane Nelsen (Sunrise Press, 1987, $7.95)

❑ *The Developing Child, Two to Six: The Play Years* by Judith K. Schneider (C.A.P.E., 1987, $6.95)

❑ *The Early Childhood Years: The Two to Six Year Old* by Theresa and Frank Caplan (Butnam Pub. Group, 1984, $4.50)

❑ *The Magic Years* by Selma H. Fraiberg (Charles Scribner, 1959, $6.95)

❑ *Your Child Is a Person: A Psychological Approach to Parenthood Without Guilt* by Stella Chess, Alexander Thomas, and Herbert G. Birch (Penguin Publishing, 1977, $3.95)

✔ Also see resources under "Discipline"

Q **What are the most important child-rearing ideas we should keep in mind now to prepare our children to live successfuly in the 21st century?**

A **We need to give childhood back to children.** The joys of chasing a butterfly and licking a bowl of chocolate frosting remain in our memories of childhood. These experiences were simple and harmed no one. They were inexpensive forms of pleasure, but they were sensuous and satisfying.

A great majority of children are burdened with adult responsibilities. Young children look after themselves before their parents return from work. Some children of working parents need to prepare dinner on a regular basis. Children need to be extra watchful that strangers and sex offenders leave them alone. Parents are educating their 6- and 7-year-olds regarding AIDS. Many children are coping with parental divorce or adjusting to stepparents while the threat of drugs and a nuclear holocaust hovers over all children.

To make matters more confusing, a number of parents are caught up in a myth that if a child learns a skill earlier, it is better. No research evidence can support that theory. Yet, parents pressure infants to toilet train themselves, toddlers to swim and preschoolers to read.

Dr. David Elkind, who is a professor of child study, a resident scholar at Tufts University and president of the 55,000-member National Association for the Education of Young Children, says that parents are "mis-educating" their preschoolers. Not only is what they are doing unnecessary but it is harmful. According to Elkind, studies have long shown that preschool children learn through play and that formal learning, if introduced too early, inhibits play and destroys the spontaneous curiosity of the child. He stresses that decades of research on intellectual readiness for mastering reading and arithmetic show that older children can master skills better and with more ease. According to Dr. Elkind, no formal lessons are necessary for preschoolers.

During early childhood, parents are needed to nurture, to protect, to provide resources. Children will then be prepared for the 21st century.

Mira Bakhle

A **Children need love, support, guidance and discipline. The major goal in raising children is, and always has been, to help them become competent, caring human beings able to function in society. This is a long 18- to 20-year process.**

Children need to develop a sense of self-worth; if they feel good about themselves, they will not be overly critical or blaming of themselves or others.

A sound educational foundation is important. Proficiency in reading, arithmetic, spelling and writing will be necessary in an ever increasing technological world.

As our children grow, it will be important for them to be able to accept change with a degree of comfort and to be flexible. They will need to have a strong sense of values as the society will be more complex than it is today. Many moral and ethical issues will confront them.

Try to provide your children with a variety of wholesome experiences. Give them the opportunity to interact with people different from themselves: elderly people, people of other racial and ethnic groups, people of different religions.

Children need to experience the world and all the wonderful things it has to teach, but this must be done gradually and with your love and support all along the way.

Dorothy Kispert

❑ *A Good Enough Parent* by Bruno Bettelheim (Knopf, 1987, $18.95)

❑ *The Hurried Child* by David Elkind (Addison-Wesley, 1981, $11.95)

❑ *Miseducation: Preschoolers at Risk* by David Elkind
(Knopf, 1987, $16.95; paperback, $7.95)

❑ *Performance Without Pressure* by Martin L. Seldman
(Walker, 1988, $17.95)

❑ *Talk With Your Child: How to Develop Reading and Language Skills
through Conversation at Home* by Harvey S. Weiner (Viking, 1988, $16.95)

Critical Thinking

If our children are to survive in an ever-changing and complex world, they
must learn the "critical-thinking" skills which will enable them to approach
a problem logically and confidently. The following suggestions are from the
U.S. Department of Education's Office of Educational Research and Improvement:

▲ **Help children develop a problem-solving framework.** The approach will
differ from child to child, but it will involve 1.) defining the problem; 2.)
making a plan to solve it; 3.) identifying possible solutions and evaluating
them.

▲ **Encourage children to go beyond the given;** not merely taking for
granted that something is accurate just because they read it in a book or
newspaper. If it doesn't make sense, challenge it; go to other sources.

▲ **Have them make comparisons.** Making comparisons stimulates thinking.
With a five-year-old, it might be categories of food; with a teenager,
musicians.

▲ **Encourage Invention.** Allow your children to think of better (or at least
different) ways of performing tasks. Don't merely answer their questions,
ask them some in return.

▲ **Use "guided imagery" to gain insights into your child's thinking.** This
technique uses all five senses as your child tries to imagine (make an
"image") of an event or experience – both past and future.

Q My 5-year-old son is afraid to go to sleep. He has nightmares of monsters. He wets the bed because he is afraid to go to the bathroom. He cries when I make him sleep in his own room. Should I let him sleep with me?

A Childhood sleep disturbances can often immobilize a family. Everyone, including your child, becomes helpless because they can't figure out what to do.

Dr. Richard Ferber, an authority on sleep problems, cautions parents to recognize that their child's fears may not make any sense but they are very real and frightening to the child. It is critical that you try to be understanding, sympathetic and comforting without being punishing and overly harsh in voice or action. Dr. Ferber believes that it is your child's "urges," "worries" and "fears" which are the real problems requiring understanding.

When something is upsetting, a child often needs to make up a reason like monsters to explain what is really causing him a problem. Searching the room, looking under the bed, going through closets, etc. basically gives credence to the fear that monsters may actually exist. Try limiting that approach.

It will be comforting for your son to know that you are in control of your own emotions and it is O.K. for him to worry or to be angry. A predictable bedtime routine will also comfort and reassure him.

Allowing your son to sleep with you does little to promote his sense of independence and security about separating from you. He can also become overly stimulated. He may develop too great a sense of power knowing that he can come between you and your husband, especially if one of you sleeps some place else while the other makes room for him in your bed.

Steven Spector

A It is natural for young children to experience fear of the dark. As they grow, children are given more responsibilities that ask them to venture into dark rooms to fetch things and to go to the bathroom at night. These are opportunities for children to learn to trust themselves and their environment.

Remember the purpose of sleep. Sleep should never be viewed as a method of punishment or discipline. However, sometimes children feel abandoned and left out, or that their parents are glad to be rid of them for the night. Establish a nurturing bedtime routine. Invest the time in reading before bed, telling stories and sharing events that happened to both of you during the day. Think of something positive that will happen the next day, and let your youngster practice closing his eyes to see if he can visualize it. These exercises in imagination are restful and fun, and can reduce the anxiety of bedtime.

Let your son come with you to choose a night light, and have a flashlight near his bed. Your children's librarian can provide a long list of bedtime books about monsters in closets and under the bed. You might remove any monster-like posters or stuffed animals for a while. For some children these objects are quite menacing. Create a chart that records success with stickers or stars and applaud this success as you would any other developmental accomplishment.

Letting your child sleep with you because it is easier will only add to your exhaustion. A caring, creative and consistent approach will bring long-term results and will build self-esteem.

Gerryann Olson

Resources

❏ *Solve Your Child's Sleep Problems* by Richard Ferber (Simon & Schuster, 1986. $7.95)

❏ *Annie Stories: A Special Kind of Storytelling* by Doris Brett (Workman Publishing, 1989, $5.95) *ED NOTE: Helps children control fears through the power of imagination.*

❏ **Taming Monsters, Slaying Dragons:** *The Revolutionary Family Approach to Overcoming Childhood Fears and Anxieties* by Joel Feiner and Graham Yost (Arbor House, 1988, $17.95)

❏ **The Magic Years** by Selma H. Fraiberg (Charles Scribner's Sons,1959, $6.95)
ED NOTE: Don't be put off by the publication date. This book is a classic which takes parents into the mind of the young child.

❏ **Sweet Dreams for Little Ones:** *Bedtime Fantasies to Build Self-Esteem* by Michael Pappas (Winston Press, $7.45)

Q My child was 2 when her father died. Now she is 6 and I'd like to talk to her about her daddy, whom I loved very much. Can you help me to explain death to her?

A Children do not understand that death is permanent until they are 8 or 9 years old. Then they are aware that the person who died is gone and will not return. But children will ask questions such as: "Where did he go?" "Will he be hungry?" "Will he be afraid of the dark?" "Will he miss us?" It reassures the child to be told the person who died will not feel frightened and lonely.

Children may be frightened if they are told that the person went to sleep, because then they may be afraid of the dark and going to sleep. Children are comforted with the concept of heaven where the person is at peace. It helps them to know that the person who died was loved. It also helps for you to talk about the fact that the individual who died was an adult, that the death occurred in adulthood and does not usually happen to children.

Since your daughter was 2 when her father died and now she is 6, she has had the experience of being cared for by you alone for four years. This in itself is very reassuring. Childrens' greatest fear is that they will be abandoned and left alone. They need to hear that they will be well cared for. Tell your daughter that you have taken care of her since her father died and that you will continue to do so for a long time – until she is "grown up."

Reassure your daughter that she had nothing to do with the death of her father. She also needs to hear how much you loved your husband and how much he loved each of you.

Each year as your daughter grows you can share more about your husband's life and answer more of her questions.

Joseph Fischoff

A Explaining death to young children is difficult because death is an emotionally charged subject and uncomfortable to talk about. Parents, however, can provide comfort and reassurance by describing death in a simple, straight-forward manner and by acknowledging the sadness people feel when a loved one dies.

When you explain your husband's death to your 6-year-old daughter, remember that understanding is limited to age and developmental stage. At 6, a child's thinking is very concrete and literal, so words need to be carefully chosen to prevent misunderstandings. At this age children continue to use magical thinking. They make up what they can't understand. They are just beginning to understand that death is permanent. Therefore, avoid statements like: "Your daddy has gone away" or "We lost your daddy," because she may conclude he will "come back" or be "found." Rather, tell her that daddy became very sick or was badly hurt in a terrible accident and that he was so sick/hurt that his body "stopped working" and he died.

Your daughter may have several questions about what it is like to be dead and you can answer: "When someone dies he can't eat, play, work or feel things." She may also be worried that you will die and she will be alone. Provide reassurance by saying that you are young and healthy and not likely to die until after she is grown-up and has children of her own. Also, name other family members who love and could care for her.

Your daughter can get to know her father through you. Tell her what he said the day she was born, how much he loved her and the things they did together when he was still alive. As she gets older you can share the memories you have and the things about him that made you love and marry him.

Patricia T. Siegel

For parents:

☐ *"A Death in the Family"* (#FL 542) by Elizabeth Ogg ($1.00)
Public Affairs Pamphlets
381 Park Avenue S., New York, NY 10016-8884

☐ *How Do We Tell the Children:* A Parent's Guide to Helping Children
Understand and Cope When Someone Dies
by Dan Schaefer and Christine Lyons (New Market, 1986, $14.95)

☐ *Helping Children Cope With Death* by Rev. Robert V. Dodd
(Herald Press, 1984, $1.95)

☐ *Learning to Say Goodbye:* When A Parent Dies by Edna Le Shan
(Avon, 1978, $3.95)

☐ *On Children and Death* by Elisabeth Kubler-Ross (MacMillan, 1985, $4.95)

For the whole family:

☐ *The Fall of Freddie the Leaf:* With a New Beginning Living Through Loss
by Leo Buscaglia. (Nightingale-Conant, 1987, $7.95, Audio Book)

For children:

☐ *Blackberries In the Dark* by Mavis Jukes (Knopf, 1985, $10.95)
About death of a grandparent. For grades 4 - 6.

☐ *Family Secrets:* Five Very Important Stories by Susan Shreve
(Knof, 1979, $6.95) About suicide of a friend. For grades 4 - 6.

☐ *The Killer Swan* by Eth Clifford (Houghton Mifflin, 1980, $6.95)
About suicide of parent. For grades 4 - 6.

☐ *The Kid's Book About Death and Dying* by Eric Rofes
(Little Brown, 1985, $14.95)

✔ For young adults, see "Suicide" resources in *Contemporary Issues* section.

Q Many people think spanking is wrong. But when I can't figure out any other way to teach my 3-year-old to stay out of the street or to stop climbing on furniture, I resort to spanking. I'm trying to raise a responsible child. Are there other effective methods of discipline?

A Saying, "Stay away from the street," will not work. Exploring is the serious business of the 3-year-old. They touch, smell, taste everything in sight. This is how they learn. Close supervision is a must because they are not aware of danger. Physically removing your child from potential danger in a firm manner conveys to the child that you care about him. It teaches right from wrong.

Three-year-olds learn though play. You can help your child to dramatize a dangerous situation and pretend how to avoid it. Through this play your youngster will understand what he can and cannot do. He will begin to develop a set of values.

Spanking is disrespectful and undignified. It destroys your relationship with your child and leaves many invisible scars.

Mira Bakhle

A Spanking is a delicate issue. One tendency abusive parents have in common is poor emotional control. If you find yourself overreacting to how your child is behaving, the problem may not be your child, but you.

There is no easy answer in raising a 3-year-old. It's your responsibility to make your child's world as safe as possible. If you are trying to teach your child not to climb on the furniture, provide something else to climb on which is safe. Or buy easily-washed slip covers.

Guadalupe Lara

✔ **For counseling referral,** call your local **Department of Social Services,** listed under "Michigan, State of" in the white pages of your phone directory. Your school principal, local United Way or United Community Services can also be of assistance.

❏ *Child Care: Parent Care* by Marilyn Heins and Anne Seiden (Doubleday, 1987, $17.95)
ED NOTE: A fine book, written by physicians who are mothers.

❏ **Toddlers and Parents** by T. Barry Brazelton (Dell, 1986, $10.95)

❏ **Your Three-Year-Old** by Louise B. Ames and Frances Ilg (Dell, 1980, $7.95)

❏ *Child Discipline:* Guidelines for Parents by Gary May (1987, $2.50) National Committee for Prevention of Child Abuse 332 S. Michigan Ave., Suite 950, Chicago, IL 60604-4357

❏ **Systematic Training For Effective Parenting (S.T.E.P.) Handbook** by Don Dinkmeyer and Gary McKay (Random House, 1983, $9.95)

■ **"What You Should Know About Disciplining Your Child"** is free from The Child Abuse and Neglect Council of Oakland County 50 Wayne St., #204, Pontiac, MI 48058 Contact the Child Abuse Council in your county for pamphlets available. Other titles include: "About Parenting," "What Everyone Should Know About Child Neglect," "What Everyone Should Know About Child Abuse," "Sobre El Maltrato De Los Ninos" and "Child Sexual Abuse Prevention Tips to Parents."

■ *Spare the Rod,* a Footsteps Film. Inquire at your Intermediate School District or Regional Educational Media Center (REMC) offices.

✔ Also see other "Discipline" questions and "Child Abuse" resources.

Q When I was growing up children were "seen and not heard" and they were punished with a good spanking when the situation warranted. My daughter-in-law seems very lenient with my grandchildren. Aren't there any strict disciplinarians left?

A Attitudes about discipline have changed. Spanking and other forms of physical discipline are now advised only under life-threatening situations, if ever.

It is very easy to overuse spanking, so that the child learns that physical force is the way to handle any dispute. The child then uses the same type of force on others, especially those younger or less powerful. The parent can easily, when upset, use force bordering on child abuse.

Children who were "seen and not heard" learned that adults did not understand and respect them, and that the only way adults could handle them was by denigrating them.

Disciplining children and listening to children is not easy. Each parent must thoughtfully work out the methods that work with his own child. What worked in the past, or even what works with one's relatives, may only have worked "in spite of" and not "because of."

Parents who can understand, communicate with, – and especially respect – their children, will most likely later have a grown child who understands, communicates with, and respects the parent..

E. Bryce Alpern

Resources

❑ *Between Parent and Child* by Haim G. Ginott (Avon, 1969, $3.95)

❑ *Experts Advise Parents:* A Guide to Raising Loving Responsible Children
edited by E. Shiff (Delacorte Press, 1987, $9.95)

❑ *Loving Your Child Is Not Enough:* Positive Discipline That Works
by Nancy Samalin with Martha Jablow (Viking, 1987, $15.95)

✔ Also see resources listed under other "Discipline" questions, "Parent
Education" and "Family Conflict" in this section.

Positive Discipline

**If begun at an early age and followed consistently, these guidelines from
the National PTA can be of ongoing value in helping parents instill both
discipline and feelings of self-worth in their children:**

▲ **Set a good example.** Children learn more from how parents behave than
from what they say.

▲ **Put limits on your children's behavior, but be careful not to make too
many rules,** and eliminate unnecessary rules as children grow older; this
will encourage independence.

▲ **Be consistent.** A few rules that are always enforced are more effective
than many rules that are enforced sporadically.

▲ **Praise children's good behavior and accomplishments.** Try to ignore
bad behavior unless it is destructive, dangerous or harmful to others.

▲ **Take time to listen to your children,** especially if they have a problem.

▲ **Encourage independence in your children.** Help them learn that they
can cope without you.

▲ **Let children contribute to the making of family rules and decisions.**
They are less likely to break rules they have helped to make.

▲ **Make sure children understand the household rules** – and penalties.

▲ **Act quickly when a child misbehaves.** Don't let a behavioral problem
drag on endlessly without attention or resolution.

▲ **Avoid power struggles with your children.** Discipline is not a game in
which there are winners and losers.

▲ **Keep your sense of humor.** It can work wonders with your children and
help you keep your perspective about what is really important.

▲ **Treat your children as you would your best friends** – build your
relationships on a foundation of respect, courtesy and love.

The National PTA –88 Back-to-School Guide for Parents, Redbook Supplement

Q My kids bicker and are rude and cruel. How can I prevent this fighting?

A A family is a system – somewhat like a spider web, where each strand holds the web together. How does your family deal with hassles and getting what they want? Your children may be fighting because that's the way the family acts.

Some families struggle against, rather than with, daily annoyances. The struggle is acted out by the children.

Your kids may only know how to try out different ways of living by fighting and bickering. You can help them to express their feelings and defend their rights without being overbearing and acting out their anger. Do this by explaining carefully and watching your behavior.

Make sure one child doesn't always get picked on or start the fight; stop any bullying that is going on. Sometimes bickering is pretty natural in growing up. But in other cases, the fighting, bickering and rudeness mean real problems and family counseling is needed.

Paul Pearsall

A When kids fight and bicker all the time, parents soon begin to think of this type of behavior as normal. Parents then communicate to the children that they are overwhelmed and no longer in control. This can cause the children to fight and bicker even more.

You can't lump all the fighting and bickering together. Look at each incident. One child may have good reason to defend himself. Listen hard to what is being said and observe carefully what is going on. Think about what your own reactions would be if you were in that situation.

You need to lay down the rules and show that you are the boss. Communicate with them in a way that will let them know you are rejecting their behavior, not them.

Guadalupe Lara

❏ *How to Talk So Kids Will Listen and Listen So Kids Will Talk*
by A. Faber and E. Mazlish (Avon, 1982, $5.95)

❏ *Parent Awareness Training: Positive Parenting for the 1980's*
by Saf Lerman (Harper & Row, 1981, $7.95)

❏ *What Every Child Would like His Parents to Know to Help Him With His Emotional Problems of Everyday Life* by Lee Salk
(Simon & Schuster, 1984, $8.95)

❏ *When Your Child Drives You Crazy* by Edna Le Shan
(St. Martins, 1985, $14.95)

❏ *Who's In Control? A Parent's Guide to Discipline*
by S. Issacs and S.F. Stoll. (Putnam, 1986, $5.95)

✔ Also see "Sibling Rivalry."

Q My husband can't say "I love you" to our children. He says they know. What should I do?

A Young children have a special sense for knowing when they are being respected and loved, without words and hugging. They also know when they are put down and ignored.

Your husband may be reacting to "love your children" as if he is being told to take out the trash. He may be digging in his heels and feeling resentful.

Make room for each child and your husband to be alone for two- to four-hour trips (no one else and no movies). The zoo, sledding, a museum -- they name it. Even if they don't talk, your child will remember for the rest of his life. Do it regularly and don't be jealous. Your child will get the love message all right.

John M. Dorsey, Jr.

A Deep down, young kids feel better if Daddy says directly, "I love you." But there are other ways to express it - hugging, kissing, the love in our voice, being available.

I'd talk to the father and explain that children under seven understand love best when he says "I love you." If that doesn't work, explain to the kids that Daddy really loves them when he gives them a bath or reads a book. It's his way of loving without words. You'll have to do the talking; it's important to kids.

Neil Kalter

Resources

❑ *101 Ways to Tell Your Child "I Love You"* by Vicki Lansky
(Contemporary Books, 1988, $4.95)

❑ *Daddy Cool* by Hugh O'Neil (Warner Books, 1988, $6.95)

❑ *Dimensions of Fatherhood*
by Shirley M.H. Hanson & Frederick W. Bozett
(Sage Publications, 1985, $16.95)

❑ *Parents Book for New Fathers* by David Laskin
(Ballantine Books, 1988, $4.50)

❑ *Single Fathers* by Geoffrey Grief (Lexington Books, 1985, $8.95)

❑ *The Father's Almanac* by S. Adams Sullivan
(Doubleday & Co., 1980, $13.95)

❑ *The Father's Book* by Carol Kort and Ronnie Friedland
(G.K. Hall & Co., 1986, $9.95 paperback.)

❑ *The Nurturing Father* by Kyle D. Pruett. (Warner Books, 1987, $18.95)

✔ **Lullabyes for Fathers** is a cassette collection of bedtime songs especially
for fathers and children. ($19.95 + $3.50 shipping and handling)
Jazz Plus, Inc. 130 Fayette St., Ithaca, NY 14850

✔ *Nurturing Today* is a quarterly publication focusing oin the family. Includes
a regular section on fathering.
David L. Giveans, Publisher
187 Casewell Ave., San Francisco, CA 94114

▲ **National Congress For Men**
3715 Brewerton Road, N. Syracuse, NY 13212
(315) 455-7043 or (315) 638-4216

Q My husband's employer offers several different medical insurance plans to choose from – including an HMO. How can I tell which health care plan would be best for my family?

A The economics of medical care for children have changed and are continuing to change. Many families, especially where one parent is employed by a large company, now have a choice of methods for paying for health care.

The traditional method includes partial or complete payment of the hospital and the physician while the patient is in the hospital. Some insurance will also cover some office visits or office surgery and drugs. This method gives the most freedom of choice.

With the second method, the **Health Maintenance Organization**, physicians are usually employees of the HMO and the care is given at special sites, clinic buildings and specified hospitals. There is often limited choice of the medical provider.

With the third type, the **Private Practitioners' Organization**, physicians usually practice in their own offices. They must join the PPO so the patient's choice is more limited. The provider is paid from a fund created from payments by the employer.

There are many variations of medical insurance plans within each of these three groups. Answers to these questions may help families decide:

1. What is the basic philosophy of the plan – giving good medical care or saving money?

2. Among the physicians available, do I have a choice for primary care and for specialist care?

3. Who decides if my child may see a specialist? Is the specialist available only on the decision of the primary physician or can I decide?

4. Which hospitals will be used for inpatient care? Where are they located?

5. What laboratory tests, x-rays or other tests are covered? Is the choice of tests only that of the primary physician or do I have input?

6. How much time is spent with each child? How busy is the physician? How long must I wait to see him or her?

7. Must I go to different offices or can I have all our children's care done at one place?

8. Is it difficult to change physicians?

9. How available is the physician after hours?

E. Bryce Alpern

Resources

❏ The Doctor Book: A Nuts and Bolts Guide to Patient Power by Wesley J. Smith (Price, Stern, Sloan, 1987, $7.95) Introduction by Ralph Nader, has nearly 30 pages devoted to selecting a health care plan.

❏ *Taking Charge of Your Medical Fate* by Lawrence C. Horowitz (Random House, 1988, $18.95)
ED NOTE: Dr. Horowitz was staff director of the U.S. Senate Subcommittee on Health and Scientific Research. He asserts in his book that "There is an oversupply of doctors and it's a patient's market...so shop around for the best health care."

Q Our child seems to be emotionally disturbed. We can't afford treatment at a private clinic. What mental health services does the state provide?

A Michigan has 55 Community Mental Health (CMH) Service Boards which provide guidance, counseling, diagnosis and treatment to those of any age suffering from emotional distress or mental illness. You can find the phone number of your local community mental health agency by calling for information at your county offices.

If problems should arise with your child, call your local CMH Board for an appointment to discuss the issues and decide on a course of care. If you can't afford to pay, there are no charges for this service or any of the others that may be provided as part of a helping program. Help may be provided directly by the CMH staff or arrangements may be made for referral to appropriate private or non-profit resources more convenient to you.

You are certainly wise to pay close attention to your child's development. Seeking a little help early on may prevent the necessity of a lot of help at a later date. Most problems, if dealt with early, can be managed in relatively brief time periods with a child remaining in school and at home.

Many counties now have the capacity to provide care in the child's own residence. If difficulties become more severe, there are many other possibilities which might include brief hospitalization or even temporary placement outside the home.

Your local Community Mental Health Center is also able to provide families with help in other areas:

Developmentally Disabled - All CMH Boards have extensive service for children who are epileptic, retarded, those with cerebral palsy or with significant birth defects. These services include, among other things: in-home care and training, day programs that prepare for employment and improve daily functioning, family counseling, respite care, and when necessary, out-of-home placement.

Adult Services - In addition to diagnosis and medication, services include day programs for occupational and recreational purposes, counseling services, help with residential difficulties and support services for young adults living outside their family home.

Elderly - CMH can help families deal with the problems of elder parents or grandparents who acquire physical and mental disabilities common to old age.

While we do not yet have in all counties enough of the kinds of programs we need, there is a well-developed array of private services and a growing network of public ones. The latter do not charge the users of the service if they are unable to pay. *No citizen of Michigan, because of lack of money, need go without care.*

James H. Graves

Resources

▲ **Michigan Association for Emotionally Disturbed Children**
(313) 356-2566, 8:30-4:30 M-F

❏ *The Growing Years:* The New York Hospital–Cornell Medical Center Guide to Your Child's Emotional Development from Birth to Adolescence with Mark Rubinstein, M.D. (Atheneum, 1988, $22.95)

❏ *Surviving Schizophrenia: A Family Manual* by E. Torrey (Harper & Row, 1984, $19.95)

❏ *Schizophrenia:* Straight Talk for Family and Friends by M. Walsh (Morrill, 1985, $17.95)

Q Can a six-week parenting course featuring discipline, self-esteem, family relationships and communications really help my family?

A Yes, six classes can make a difference. Do you see the seeds of rebellion in your kids? Are they doing poorly in school? Are you losing the battle for control and influence? The course can provide a fresh start – in the direction of a loving relationship, free of power struggles.

Consider this true story: A daughter came to her mom in tears, clutching an heirloom afghan. When she unfolded the afghan, soaking wet from cleaning efforts, she displayed two huge blotches of nail polish. The mother wanted to let loose with scolding and shaming remarks. But the mother, a parenting class member, observed that the child was already overcome with guilt and sorrow. Scolding would have crushed the child's spirit and poisoned their relationship.

The mother later said, "If the class did nothing but get us through that moment, it was worth it."

Dennis Nordmoe

A In selecting family-living courses, use guidelines:

- Is the purpose specific and clear?

- Are presenters' credentials listed and relevant? A graduate degree does not automatically make a parent educator.

- You need to practice to learn parenting skills. Successful teachers spend several sessions on one specific topic such as discipline; they aren't "all over the map."

- Chronic and specific problems are best addressed in therapy; general family issues can be approached in a course.

- Attend with a spouse/friend. Discuss what you have learned.

- Keep in mind that there is no research to support one exclusive style of parenting.

- Be sure you get an overview of current research findings and that the research is clear to you.

- Discussion periods are helpful. Avoid parent education that is only books and tapes. This is "selling not telling!"

- Form a neighborhood group, including older children. Select your own materials, invite qualified speakers. Then you may have the most effective parent education of all.

Paul Pearsall

Resources

Training Materials for Parenting Workshops
The following training materials and curriculum programs are available for workshops and seminars given by schools, churches, community organizations and neighborhood parent groups.

Michigan Programs

✔ **A survey of parenting programs and services** offered in 1988 has been compiled by Gov. James Blanchard's Human Services Cabinet Council. Parents can find out where programs are in their county by contacting:
Patricia L. Hebert, Ph.D.,
Human Service Cabinet Council, Office of the Governor
P.O. Box 30013, Lansing, MI 48909
(517) 335-4480

■ **Detroit Family Project**, a program for urban parents being developed by the Detroit Department of Health and the Council on Early Childhood at Wayne State University's Center for Urban Studies
College of Urban, Labor, Metropolitan Affairs
For information, contact Charlene Firestone, project coordinator.
(313) 577-2208

■ **Getting Involved: Workshops for Parents** by Ellen Frede
High/Scope Educational Research Foundation
600 North River Street, Ypsilanti, MI 48197
(313) 485-2000

- **Parent Talk** with columnist and broadcaster Evelyn Petersen. Series of 60-minute audio cassettes for discussion group or individual use. Tapes by age group (2- to 5-year-olds, school-age and teens) answer questions most asked by parents. $10.00 per tape; quantity discounts.
  Parent Talk, 843 S. Long Lake Rd., Traverse City, MI 49684
  (616) 943-9257

- **The Caring Parent**, a program serving parents in the Detroit Public Schools. Contact Ethel Washington at (313) 494-1660.

- *Strengthening and Supporting Families: A Parent Education Curriculum* from the Michigan Department of Social Services (1987, $10.00)
  Council on Early Childhood, Center for Urban Studies
  Wayne State University, Detroit, MI 48202

National Programs

- **Active Parenting,** based on work of Michael H. Popkins; video tape series featuring *Parenting Styles, Understanding Your Child, Instilling Courage, Developing Responsibility, Winning Cooperation* , and *Dynamics of the Democractic Family.* Includes workbook, leader's guide and parent handbook.
  4669 Roswell Rd. N.E., Atlanta, GA 30342
  1-800-235-7755

- **Children the Challenge,** developed by Rudloph Driekers, deals with raising a responsible child, family relations, listening skills, discipline and coping skills, and acheiving mutual respect between parent and child.
  Alfred Adler Institute, 159 N. Dearborn St., Chicago, IL 60601

- **Nurturing Program** by Stephen J. and Julianna Dillinger Bavolek (1985)
  Family Development Resources, Inc.
  767 Second Avenue, Eau Claire, WI 54703

- **Parenting, the Undeveloped Skill:** *A Joint Project of the National PTA and the March of Dimes* (1986, $6.00 to PTA members, $8.00 others)
  National PTA, P.O. Box 1015 Tinley Park, IL 60477

- **Systematic Training for Effective Parenting (STEP)** and other parenting programs such as *Active Parenting, Assertive Discipline, Marriage Enrichment, Responsive Parenting, STEP, PECES (Spanish edition), STEP/Teen, STEP Biblically, The Next STEP Video, Sexual Abuse Prevention, Teen Development.*
  American Guidance Services, Publisher's Building
  Circle Pines, MN 55014-1796 ; 1-800-328-3560

■ **The University of Minnesota's film and video collection of educational materials is one of the largest in the country.** Fifty-three pages of annotated films and videos available to professionals and families. Rentals from $15.00-$40.00. Request their **Family System catalogue.**
University Film and Video, University of Minnesota, 1313 Fifth St. S.E.
Suite 108, Minneapolis, MN 55414
1-800-847-8251, 7:45-4:30 CST, M-F

❏ *Black Parenting: Strategies for Training* by Kirby Alvey.
(Irvington Publishers Inc., 1987, $29.95.)
Center for Improvement of Child Caring
11331 Ventura Blvd., Studio City, CA 91604.

✔ Also see resources next question.

Q My kids are like little demons. They know just how to "get me," but I'm not whacking them yet. I just do a lot of yelling. I got hit a lot when I was growing up and I still remember how awful that was. I need more help to understand my children.

A Some parents think of discipline as gaining control over the child. That's why they hit and spank. These parents mistakenly feel that hurting children teaches respect. What hitting does teach is resentment, anger, fear, even hatred. Each time you discipline ask yourself what your youngster learned from how he was disciplined. This will give you a whole new way of looking at what is going on in your family.

Consult some of the resources listed in this section for further guidance.

Ann Soderman

A To discipline is to teach. To punish is to hurt. Our goal in parenting is to help children grow independent from us through teaching them how to behave in a mature manner. Hitting, yelling, "the cold, silent treatment" and other cruel methods of punishment teach youngsters that we are bigger and stronger, but not much else.

Parents usually learn their parenting skills from their parents or relatives. Sometimes these are good models. Sometimes they are not in tune with understanding today. We know agreat deal more about how to help develop mature, responsible, capable children than we did a generation ago.

Parenting programs which teach parents how children develop and learn have helped many families. Such programs as S.T.E.P. (Systematic Training for Effective

Parenting) are broadly available. Check with your school, religious institutions, probate court system, community mental health board or family service agency to locate classes. Some examples are listed below.

Eli Saltz

Parenting Programs

✔ A survey of parenting programs and services offered in 1988 has been compiled by Gov. James Blanchard's Human Services Cabinet Council. Parents can find out where programs are in their county by contacting: Patricia L. Hebert, Ph.D., Human Service Cabinet Council Office of the Governor, P.O. Box 30013, Lansing, MI 48909 (517) 335-4480

Detroit/Wayne County

☎ **Telhelp** – **(313) 226-9448 or 1-800-552-1183** toll-free in Oakland, Wayne Macomb counties, 8:30 - 5 M-F

■ **Child Care Coordinating Council** of Detroit/Wayne County (4-Cs) Referrals to programs in Detroit and Wayne County. 579-2777, 8:30 - 4:30 M-F

Grand Rapids/Kent County

■ **"First Call"** – (616) 459-2255. Referral source for parenting programs.

Macomb County

■ **The Parent Family Training Program** Substance Abuse Information Center Approximately 29 S.T.E.P. and other programs available. (313) 791-5544, 8:30 a.m. - 9: p.m. M, T, T; till 6 W; till 5 F

Oakland County

■ **Oakland County Youth Assistance** (Probate Court-sponsored) has 28 Parent Education committees. Programs vary from S.T.E.P. to national parent educators. For the Youth Assistance Worker in your community, call: (313) 858-0055, 8:30-5 M-F

■ **Oakland Family Services** has several programs for pregnant women and parents of young children and infants. Program and child care free. Call Mitzi Wilcher at (313) 858-7766, 9-5 M, T, F; till 8 p.m.T-W

Q I am black. How would you advise me to bring up my two children when I know they will face bigotry and prejudice during their lifetime?

A There are basic values, attitudes, and behavioral patterns which children would do well to adopt at an early age. I encourage you to model and teach your children...

...to be wise consumers. Since racism limits the purchasing power of some, wise economic decision-making is essential. Teach your children the disciplines necessary to defer gratification. Media advertisements must not determine our children's demands for clothing, toys and candy. Even when these things are affordable, children should know that self-worth is based upon a positive sense of who we are internally, not upon fancy clothes, expensive jewelry and uncontrolled spending habits.

...to make choices. For example, involvement in illegal activities may produce quick-bucks, but is ultimately detrimental. Teach your children to make choices that produce lasting benefits for themselves, their family and community.

...to respect themselves, to be polite, to act mannerly, to use speech and engage in behavior that wins the respect of their responsible peers and elders.

...that it is OK to feel angry. Feelings are always right. But beautiful people handle feelings, including anger, in socially productive ways. Our children need not protest and decry everything that rubs them the wrong way. A great factor in the art of living beyond survival in a racist culture is the art of knowing what to overlook. Responsible parents teach their children to choose battles which the child can best fight given the situational context of the issue needing attention.

...a relevant work ethic. There are no "freebies" for minorities in a racist society. Doing just enough to "get by" is a creeping form of suicide. Teach your children to work smart, as well as hard. It is not always the early bird who gets the worm. Oftentimes it's the smart bird who knows where to scratch and how to dig. Doing one's homework well and seeking always to be informed are lifelong, enjoyable and profitable tasks.

...**finally, surround your children with adequate role models and reference groups.** Frequent association with appropriate company help compromise the dehumanizing influences that impact children. The church could serve as one such reference group. Another group could include responsible persons whom you select to function as members of your extended family.

Robert O. Dulin, Jr.

A **Racism is a form of denigration based on the devaluation and dehumanization of an entire population** of people because of the color of their skin. It permeates all aspects of our society. From the time of formalized slavery to the present, whites have opposed Third World people by perpetuating racism at every level. Racism is present in our institutions, our culture and our individual actions. It is a serious and explosive issue in our country.

Racism is subtle as well as blatant. It is the day-to-day indignities, the subtle humiliations that are so devastating. Racism is the assumption of superiority of one group over another, with all the gross arrogance that goes along with it.

Racism and inaccurate information are intertwined in not so subtle ways. Racists see to it that children receive inaccurate information. Help your child learn important information about his history, and develop a sense of pride in his heritage. Unfortunately, he has to learn to defy the image that has been projected of blacks via television, history books and media. He must develop a sense of pride and personal awareness. Expose him to positive role models. Seek out black professionals with whom he can identify. Point out historical misinformation and subtle forms of racism such as TV shows that depict black men as weak and powerless.

Do not pretend that the problem does not exist. Education-al and psychological preparation are the best defenses for overcoming negative stereotypes imposed upon you by white society.

Racism is unhealthy for white children. It is unrealistic and distorted for them to grow up feeling superior to peoples of color based on the color of their skin. All families need to discuss issues of racism and expose children to racially and ethnically integrated experiences.

Donald Davis

A **Parents may not be able to stop their children from encountering racism, but their guidance can keep youngsters from accepting prejudiced beliefs** about black people and from being overwhelmed by bigotry. Studies have indicated that black children with a strong sense of racial identity are less affected by racist situations than other black children.

These steps will help you to arm your children against racism:

Learn about black history and culture and teach that information to your children. Children who are proud of their heritage are likely to believe they can succeed despite obstacles.

Teach your children how to recognize and confront racism. When parents explain racism as due to the bigot's ignorance or low self-esteem, black children are freed from unnecessary shame and guilt.

Be assertive in racist situations. A parent whose child is called a racially insulting name by another child can educate the of-fender. Don't ignore the situation because the offender didn't know any better. Your children must learn they are not help-less when hurt or hindered by prejudice.

Louise Reid Ritchie

■ **Black Family Development Inc.** offers Wayne County residents parent education training classes and counseling from a black perspective.
15231 W. McNichols, Detroit, MI 48235
(313) 272-3500, 9-5 M-F

■ **The Museum of Afro-American History**
301 Fredrick Douglas St., Detroit, MI 48202
(313) 833-9800

■ **Your Heritage House**
Exploration programs in the fine arts for children of all races.
110 East Ferry, Detroit, MI 48202
(313) 871-1667; 9-5 M-F; 10-3 Sat.

■ *Black Children: Their Roots, Culture and Style* by Janice E. Hale-Bensen (Johns Hopkins, 1986, $9.95)

Q We haven't gone to church in years, but as children, we both had formal religious training (in different faiths). Now that we are parents, we have begun to see that our religious educations played a major role in giving us a sense of morality, community and spirituality – values that we would like to impart to our own children. How do we accomplish this?

A To encourage and nurture our children's relationship with God is a necessary and tremendous boost to a child's self-concept, sense of self-worth and self-esteem. This is best done by the child's parents who out of active concern for their own faith development will necessarily model those commitments and attitudes vital to meeting one's spiritual needs. This means that the most helpful kind of "spiritual education" for our children involves more than choosing a Sunday School for our children. A more helpful and comprehensive perspective includes choosing a church that is capable of resourcing the spiritual needs of the entire family.

Children understand very little about abstract religious concepts before age 12. However, this is not to suggest that children are incapable of a meaningful relationship with God. Children tend to have a special sense for the mysterious presence of God and are quick to acknowledge their dependence on their creator. The annuals of religious education are full of stories of very young children who made serious and lasting effective commitments to God. For young children this commitment is nurtured by parents and other significant adults who represent God by everything they say and do.

Choose a church that has a viable program of religious education staffed with persons who recognize that religious education has to do with resourcing persons and families with whatever they need to achieve their highest potential.

Robert O. Dulin, Jr.

A Do you want your children to value self, but in a way that gives priority to others in need? Do you want your children to relate to the real source of life, God? Then you will start shopping – carefully – for a religious community clearly showing these values and this insight. It will take time and testing.

You will associate with this church first for your own good and support – and let it assist you in the spiritual nurturing of your children. If you only send your children to that church, you do not model serious spiritual commitment and undercut your purpose.

A great religious teacher, Paul Tillich, used to say to his students that any society (let's say "family" here) not imparting its most deeply cherished values and beliefs to its young will set in motion its own demise.

Oscar J. Ice

Resources

❑ *Bringing Up a Moral Child: A New Approach for Teaching Your Child To Be Kind, Just and Responsible* by Michael Schulman and Eva Mekler (Addison-Wesley, 1985, $12.95)

❑ *But How Will You Raise The Children? A Guide to Interfaith Marriage* by Steven Carr Reuben (Pocket Books, 1987, $6.95)

❑ *Mixed Blessings:* Marriage Between Jews and Christians by Paul Cowan and Rachel Cowan. (Doubleday, 1987, $18.95) *ED NOTE: Especially Chapter 7 - "Stepping Stones to a Family Faith."*

❑ *Raising Your Child to Be a Mensch*: *Decent, responsible, caring person* by Neil Kurshan (Atheneum, 1987, $14.95)

❑ *Values for Tomorrow's Children: An Alternative Future for Education in the Church* edited by John H. Westerhoff, III (Pilgrim Press, 1979, $5.95)

❑ Also see "Responsibility" in this section and "Media-Influence" in *Contemporary Issues.*

Q How can I help my children to learn to be responsible? What works at what age?

A Children start learning how to be responsible very early. As parents, our job is to help them learn how to make responsible choices – and to show them that doing so will make them feel good.

Responsibility includes attitudes about our belongings, work, talents and time. It affects our interactions with others. Making responsible choices all the time isn't easy, even for adults. Like it or not, our children will learn both responsibility and irresponsibility from our example.

One way children can learn to make responsible choices is by managing their own money. Until they are old enough to get paying jobs, earning a regular weekly allowance based on completing chores is one way to teach them responsibility. Here are examples of ways allowances can help:

Responsibility means usually doing what you have to do first and doing what you like to do later. Suppose your child watches TV instead of finishing certain jobs within the specified time. Cut the allowance according to how many jobs aren't done and your child will see the consequences of his or her choice.

Responsibility means setting goals and knowing what you want and why before you start. If your child wants something special like a particular toy or piece of equipment, talk about why he or she wants it and how it will be used. Help the child see there's more to the choice than just possessing the item. Let the child earn all the money so he or she understands the cost and can judge whether the item was worth it.

Responsibility means adjusting your goals to fit your talents and limitations, whether these are time, money or energy. Life teaches us either to accept this or to do what we can to change it and meet our goals. Allowances can help children set reasonable goals that match their time, money and energy.

Evelyn Petersen

A If your child expresses an interest in helping, he is old enough to learn responsibility and can be given a task according to his ability. Set a time for completion to provide him with a framework for measuring achievement and giving feedback.

Don't let a child off the hook if he fails to perform. If he falls short of the mark, make it a learning experience. Be aware of the risk in putting too much on a child, too soon. A child under 12 years old should not be given complete responsibility for important, regular tasks such as making dinner each day. But while a child lives at home, he should be expected to contribute on a daily basis.

A common pitfall for today's busy families is the parent that feels guilty and as a result, overcompensates and "does it all," while expecting nothing of the child. A parent who expects nothing will get nothing.

Practical Steps for Raising a Responsible Child :

Clear expectations are necessary to help the child focus on the objective.

Involve children when planning tasks.

Guarantee success by choosing easy tasks at first and gradually increasing the level of responsibility.

Demonstrate skills to teach a child how to do a task: "sweep like this...put pieces in the box like this."

Provide incentives for completing jobs by connecting tasks with rewards: praise, affection, increased level of responsibility, pay.

Have a positive attitude. A parent that grumbles and complains about responsibilities conveys a strong negative message.

Seek out opportunities for teamwork rather than allowing children to work in isolation. Learning how to cooperate is a valuable tool.

John Abbey

✔ *You and Money,* a learning guide for 8 -12 year olds, has puzzles, games and work sheets. (Fidelity Investments, 1988, free) 1-800-544-6666

❑ *Bringing Up a Moral Child: A New Approach for Teaching Your Child to be Kind, Just and Responsible* by Michael Schulman and Eva Mekler (Addison-Wesley, 1985, $12.95)

❑ *High Risk: Children Without a Conscience* by Ken Magid and Carol A. McKelvey (Bantam, 1987, $24.95)

❑ *Kids Who Succeed* by Beverly Neuer Feldman (Rawson Associates, 1987, $17.95)

❑ *MegaSkills: How Families Can Help Children Succeed in School and Beyond* by Dorothy Rich (Houghton Mifflin, 1988, $8.95) *ED NOTE: Excellent, practical suggestions.*

❑ *Positive Discipline: Teaching Children Self-Discipline, Responsibility, Cooperation and Problem-Solving Skills* by Jane Nelsen (Sunrise Press, 1981, $7.95)

❑ *Raising Children for Success* by Stephen Glenn with Jane Nelsen (Sunrise Press, 1987, $7.95)

❑ *Teach Your Child Decision Making* by John Clabby and Maurice Elias (Doubleday, 1987, $8.95)

❑ *The Magic Years* by Selma H. Fraiberg (Scribner, 1954, $7.95)

Q We hear a lot about the need for self-esteem. What is it and why is it important to a child's development? Can you give me some practical suggestions to increase my child's self-esteem?

A Helping children develop good self-esteem (a person's feeling of self-worth) is probably the most important thing parents can do for their children. People with high self-esteem are capable of making good decisions, proud of their accomplishments, willing to take responsibility and able to cope with frustration. They are also likely to be creative because they are willing to meet challenges and take risks in new situations.

Good feelings about oneself begin at home. When children feel that they are listened to, taken seriously and genuinely cared for, their self-esteem is high. Here are some ways parents help children to like themselves:

Reward children. Give praise, recognition, a special privilege or increased responsibility for a job well done. Emphasize the good things they do, not the bad.

Take their ideas, emotions and feelings seriously. Don't belittle them by saying, "You'll grow out of it" or "It's not as bad as you think."

Define limits and rules clearly, and enforce them. But do allow leeway for your children within these limits.

Be a good role model. Let your children know that you feel good about yourself. Also let them see that you too can make mistakes and can learn from them.

Help your children develop tolerance toward those with different values, backgrounds and norms. Point out other people's strengths.

Be available. Give support when children need it. Spend time together and share favorite activities.

Discuss problems without placing blame or commenting on a child's character. If children know that there is a problem but don't feel attacked, they are more likely to help look for a solution.

Use phrases that build self-esteem, such as "Thank you for helping" or "That was an excellent idea!" Avoid phrases that hurt self-esteem: "Why are you so stupid?" or "How many times have I told you?"

Show how much you care about them. Hug them. Tell them they are terrific and that you love them.

National PTA

A Developing your child's self-esteem is your No. 1 job. Children learn to view themselves through their parents' eyes. Self-esteem is pretty well set by 5. If I say, "She's the shy one," or, "He's no good in sports," that's exactly the way the child will develop.

Focus on the positive. Say, "You're good at picking up," or "You're terrific at sharing." When a report card has five A's and a B, say, "Five A's– this is wonderful." Later, say, "Let's see how we can turn the B into an A."

Debbie Stabenow

A Self-esteem is a by-product of accomplishment. Involve young children in simple projects like making cookies, letting them do more of the steps each time. They will always give themselves ample share of the credit! For older kids, skiing, hiking or acting accomplishes the same thing. Don't overlook the deep satisfaction that comes with long-term skill development – projects like mastering a musical instrument.

Go easy on the praise. Sometimes it can backfire, convincing children they are worthwhile only when others praise them.

Dennis Nordmoe

Q Our grandson is 4. His father sees himself in his son and inflicts on the child all the ways he was punished as a boy. We think these ways may be damaging to our grandchild's self-image. How should our son-in-law change his method of discipline and build, rather than destroy, the child's self-esteem?

A All self-esteem comes from being held in esteem the first five years of life. This period is irreplaceable for self-esteem gathering. If your grandchild is being criticized and he doesn't understand why, I would guarantee that the cycle will repeat itself again when *he* becomes a father.

Your son-in-law apparently was criticized himself as a child to a point where, in order to protect his own self-esteem, he learned not to see these problems in himself but to be critical of others for his own shortcomings. If he sees these unlikable parts of himself emerging in his son, he will be merciless, for way down deep, he hates himself and so will he hate what he sees in his son.

Many parents criticize by lowering self-esteem – "I wish you were never born," "Why can't you be like your sister?," etc. I can't emphasize how dangerous this can be. Our culture is so liberal that young people have lost the protection of a rigid society and must rely on what they think of themselves. If they like themselves, they will look out for themselves. If they don't, they won't. The father, in this case, needs counseling quickly.

John M. Dorsey, Jr.

A Many parents share your son-in-law's mistaken belief in physical punishment for children. They believe it builds moral character, fosters respect for authority, and is the antidote for the "wild youth" of the 1960s and 1970s. Research evidence does not support such beliefs.

We find that strong physical punishment is extremely frequent in the early lives of most juvenile delinquents, youthful offenders, child abusers and those being treated for drug abuse. Physical punishment increases aggressive tendencies and leads to feelings of worthlessness and rejection.

Why do the effects of physical punishment backfire? One reason is that we treat children like short adults who understand and react like adults – far from true, particularly for children under 6. Our research found that if we tried to stop children from doing something (e.g., run across the street), the louder we yelled, the more likely they were to act. A loud yell was a neurological trigger for the act. Adults would then interpret the childrens' behavior as "willful" and "disobedient" and punish.

Certainly we must civilize our children, impart our moral values, and set limits on their behavior. Taking other children's toys or hitting other children should not be tolerated. But train with love, not physical punishment. If the child takes another child's toys, return the toys calmly, and explain, "We don't do that." Children want to please; they learn from example. Sometimes the learning is slow, but it comes.

Eli Saltz

Resources

■ *Mirrors: A Film About Self-Esteem*, from the National PTA and Keebler Company, is available free to PTA units who conduct a meeting on the importance of building self-esteem. To order, write:
Scheduling Center, Modern Talking Picture Service
5000 Park St. N., St. Petersburg, FL 33709
(Submit your PTA's name, address and daytime phone number, and specify either 16 mm or 1/2 inch VHS.)

✔ **"Parenting: The Underdeveloped Skill,"** *a training program from the National PTA and March of Dimes to help parents learn to better communicate with their children and to nurture the youngsters' self-esteem. See resources under Parent Education section.*

▲ **The Importance of Self-Esteem in Children**
(part of *Choices for Positive Living* by Comerica Inc. $1.00)
ED NOTE: Contains an excellent supplemental reading list.
Mental Health Association in Michigan
15920 W. 12 Mile Rd., Southfield, MI 48076
(313) 557-6777 or 1-800-482-9534

▲ **Project Self.** Ten two-hour sessions to build self-esteem through skill-development in 12-18-year-olds.
Julie Stitt, Common Ground, 751 Hendrie, Royal Oak, MI 48067
(313) 645-1173

▲ **Self-Esteem Center,** Ray Maloney, director
Materials, counseling and workshops
725 S. Adams, L-14, Birmingham, MI 48011
(313) 258-5050

▲ **Oakland County Council For Children at Risk**
Free pamphlets including: "What You Should Know About Disciplining Your Child;" "About Parenting;" "We Work to Stop Child Abuse Before It Occurs." Contact your local Council for Children at Risk for resources.
50 Wayne St., #204, Pontiac, MI 48058; (313) 332-7173

❑ *How to Raise Children's Self-Esteem*
by Reynold Bean and Harris Clemes (Enrich, 1980, $3.95)

❑ *How's Your Family? A Guide to Identifying Your Family's Strengths and Weaknesses* by Jerry M. Lewis (Brunner-Mazel,1979, $20.00)

❑ *The Aquarian Age* by Marilyn Ferguson (J.P. Tarcher, 1981, $10.95)

❑ *The Closing of the American Mind* by Alan Bloom.
(Simon & Schuster, 1988, $5.95)

❑ *The Early Childhood Years: The Two to Six Year Old*
by Theresa and Frank Caplan (Putnam, 1983, $4.50)

❑ *The Road Less Traveled* by Scott Peck (Simon & Schuster, 1985, $16.95)

❑ *The Winning Family: Increasing Self-Esteem in Your Children and Yourself* by Louise Hart (Dodd, Mead, 1987, $7.95)

❑ *Your Child's Self-Esteem* by Dorothy C. Briggs (Doubleday, 1970, $8.95)

Q I'm concerned about the intense sibling rivalry between the 6-year-old son and the 3-year-old daughter of friends of mine. Their parents say there is "unremitting unfriendliness of the older child toward the younger."

A Sibling rivalry is very common. It is a way of testing out feelings and behaviors with someone who is safe; of finding out how to get your way and your place in the family. In most families, it is a way to practice assertiveness. It gets out of hand when children begin to use this as the major way of getting their parents' attention or when they do physical or emotional damage to one another. Parents can decrease sibling rivalry by:

giving each child lots of attention and giving each a unique and valued position in the family;

accepting children's feelings and helping them express their feelings – helping them talk about their anger;

separating the children when they aren't getting along -- don't try to figure out who started it;

having clear rules that include never physically hurting another person and bargaining to get what you want; and

avoiding comparisons as to which child is brighter, more attractive or who is the favorite.

We can't force children to like one another, but we can teach them how to treat others with respect. If there is any danger that the children are likely to hurt one another, then we must monitor their activities together in order to protect them.

Patricia Ryan

A **Sibling rivalry results when children feel that their sense of security within the family is at stake.** It's a reflection of feelings of inadequacy. They compete for parental love and attention when they feel there isn't enough to go around. As new children are added, it is natural for children to go through an adjustment as they learn to share their parents. There are several things parents can do to minimize unhealthy rivalry:

Recognize that each child is an individual with his or her own needs and personalities. Each needs love, praise, acceptance and reassurance.

Encourage a climate of cooperation. Interactions don't have to be a win-lose contest.

Don't build up one child at another's expense.

Be generous with praise, compliments and encouragement for each child – not comparing them to each other.

Teach children that a harmonious family relationship is of paramount importance. The bond between siblings is a special kind of love, caring, loyalty and protectiveness.

Don't show favoritism – overly praising or criticizing.

Encourage them to resolve their conflicts by focusing on solutions rather than blaming or demeaning each other.

Encourage positive self-concepts with emphasis on competency, and self-acceptance. Help each child appreciate his unique qualities and not strive to be his brother or sister.

K. Noelle Clark

Q My three sons, ages 8, 12, and 14, say very little to each other in a civil way. They yell, push, demean and insult each other constantly. How can I help them communicate in a civil manner and learn to respect each other?

A A certain amount of rivalry and disagreement is natural for every family. But when fighting reaches the hostile level that you have described, it is time to take a good look at the roles of each member of the family and the family interactions as a whole.

Parents have a strong impact on the kind and type of relationships that brothers and sisters develop. In order to have good communication and relationships:

Each child must feel "cared about" by the adult members of the family.

Adults in the family should not "take sides" when the children fight with one another.

Parents should set examples of good communication.

Fun family outings and family activities at home should be planned on a regular basis. These activities can teach children how to enjoy each other.

Your boys will learn to respect and like one another when they begin to enjoy being together and feel good about themselves. Open communication is a byproduct of positive relationships, high self-esteem and learned skills.

If your sons continue to fight, it would be wise to call a reliable family therapist and try to work out the problems of the family.

Helene Mills

A In families where communication is characterized by constant insults, sarcasm and hostility, children tend to look out for themselves first – even if at the expense of their sisters and brothers. It's not so much what they say that hurts, but how they say it. Sometimes an irritable tone of voice stems from habit rather than anger or real dislike. But blaming, judging and ignoring, all of which demean the worth of family members, can eventually result in less openness, less communication and less of a sense of family closeness.

Family atmosphere will be harmonious when members feel comfortable expressing their feelings in an open and honest manner. Harmony grows when the opinion of each member is respected. This leads members to be more optimistic and able to rely on each other for understanding and support.

Help your boys to practice more sensitive ways of communication with each other. Set aside a specific time each day to share feelings, events, interests and concerns. Dinner is an ideal time – without distractions such as television. Talk about big things and little things.

Encourage your sons to really listen to each other. They *will* hear each other if they pay close attention and concentrate. Listening is an active skill which you can practice with them.

Talk with your children often – encouraging them to formulate their own individual thoughts. Be aware of how you talk to them. The way parents communicate with children becomes a model for how they communicate with each other.

K. Noelle Clark

Resources

❏ *The Complete Book on Sibling Rivalry* by John McDermott (Putnam, 1987, $8.95)

❏ *Siblings Without Rivalry: How to Help Your Children Live Together So You Can Live Too* by A. Faber and E. Mazlish (Norton, 1987, $14.95)

❏ *Sibling Rivalry* by Seymour V. Reit (Ballantine Books, 1985, $3.95)

✔ Also see resources under "Discipline," "Responsibility" and "Adolescence."

Q **I have been separated from my husband for several months. We have moved three times during this period. My 7-year-old daughter misses her father desperately. She hates her school, refuses to work and complains of stomachaches. How can I help her adjust?**

A **Children in families undergoing separation have some basic needs which are often overlooked because parents don't understand their fears.** Children's unspoken fears may include worries that they will be abandoned. Children should be told from the onset where and with whom they will be living. Their new living situation should be described. Children fear that the separation or divorce is their fault or responsibility, that if they were "better" children their parents would stay together. They need to be told clearly that the separation is because mom and dad are having difficulty getting along and is not in any way their responsibility.

Children also fear that they will have to choose between their parents. They fear that one or both parents will no longer love them. Wherever possible children should be assured of a continued loving relationship with each parent and that their parents will not bad-mouth each other or try to make the child choose one over the other.

Finally, children need opportunities to express their feelings and fears to someone who can accept them and reassure them. Try talking with your daughter about some of these issues and about her feelings and concerns. If possible, involve her father in some of these discussions or ask him to talk separately with her. If she still has difficulty understanding, if she continues to be miserable, or if you have difficulty talking with her, it would be important to seek family counseling.

Carol Mitchell

A After divorce or separation young children really miss the parent with whom they spend less or very little time. Youngsters of this age also have a hard time understanding divorce. They often try to explain it to themselves by taking the blame for the divorce. They also blame themselves because the absent parent does not stay in close contact.

It may be that your daughter not only misses her father, but is also wrestling with ideas that she somehow caused the divorce and is not lovable enough for her father to want to see her a lot. If her father spends little time with her, then given her age, she could be thinking that he does not care about her anymore. That is even worse than missing him.

Try establishing or increasing regular contacts between your daughter and her father. If he does not live nearby, regular telephone calls, postcards and letters from him would be helpful. It would also be useful for you to talk with your daughter about how "kids sometimes have some mixed-up ideas about divorce, like sometimes they think maybe they caused it somehow or should have stopped it," and "kids sometimes think their dad doesn't care about them after a divorce, but dads usually do care even if they do live far away and can't see them a lot." The latter is helpful especially if the father is willing to call and write frequently.

If these strategies do not seem to alleviate your daughter's pain within three months, then it would be a good idea to consult a mental health professional. It is wise to choose a professional who is experienced in working with children whose parents have divorced. Your daughter's difficulties will be more likely to be understood as a reaction to the divorce rather than as a result of being emotionally disturbed.

Neil Kalter

Resources

✔ Contact your school principal to talk about a support group for children of separation and divorce in your child's school. *Common Ground,* 751 Hendrie, Royal Oak, MI 48067, has developed a program for schools called *Our New Family.* Call Julie Stitt at (313) 645-1173, 9-5 M-F.

✔ *"Rainbows for All God's Children,"* is a national educational program designed to assist children living in single-parent homes.
Rainbows' Michigan representative is:
Dava Szuch, 22324 Gregory, Dearborn, MI 48124; (313) 562-8499.
Periodically, Rainbow programs are offered at SPACE, a support organization for widowed, single and divorced families.
(313) 258-6606, 9-4:30 M-F

▲ **Parents Without Partners** is a national support and social group with chapters throughout Michigan. To find the one nearest you, call (313) 264-8557; (313) 722-2642; (517) 371-2525 anytime.

▲ **University Center for the Child and the Family**
Offers services on a sliding-fee basis, for as little as $7.50 per visit. The center also offers support groups for children whose parents are divorcing and support groups in schools.
University of Michigan, 1007 E. Huron St., Ann Arbor, MI 48104
(313) 764-9466, 8-8 M-T, 8-5 F

❑ *Divorce and Your Child* by Sonja Goldstein and Albert Solnit (Yale University Press, 1984, $17.50)

❑ *How It Feels When Parents Divorce* by Jill Krementz
For children age 7-16. (Knopf, 1984, $12.95)

❑ *How to Single Parent* by Fitzhugh Dodson (Harper & Row, 1987, $15.95)

❑ *Helping Children of Divorce: A Handbook for Parents and Teachers* by Susan Arnsberg Diamond (Schocken Books, 1986, $6.95)

❑ *On Divorce: An Openbook for Parents and Children Together* by Sarah Stein (Walker and Co., 1984, $4.95)

❑ *Quality Time: Easing Children Through Divorce* by Melvin G. Goldzband (McGraw-Hill, 1985, $17.95)

❑ *The Parent/Child Manual on Divorce* by Maria Sullivan (St. Martin's Press, 1988, $12.95) This and other titles available from Tom Doherty Assoc., 49 W. 24th St., New York, NY 10010

✔ Also see resources under "Divorce" in *Contemporary Issues.*

Q I'm a divorced mother with an active, well-adjusted, 9-year-old who spends almost every weekend with his father. Recently he has been complaining that the visits are boring and asking that his dad bring him home early. Neither his dad nor I can figure out why. What do you think?

A Both parents need to reassure the child that he is "special" to them. With a 9-year-old, it may be that he is becoming more attached to his peers. Perhaps a friend of your son's could accompany him and his dad on a fun trip to the farm or zoo.

Children of divorce often are anxious about having to face their parents going on a date. Even a friendly relationship can be misunderstood by a child and be interpreted as a serious involvement. Could your son's desire to return home to you be prompted by such anxieties about his dad?

Mira Bakhle

A Sometimes children use words differently than adults. Your son's definition of "boring" may not be the same as yours. He may mean that the activities are too predictable, or be complaining about not having a say in planning. Ask him, "What is it guys your age don't like on visits and what do they wish would happen?" to try to understand what is on his mind.

Occasionally we see youngsters this age preferring to spend more time with friends on weekends. Another possibility is that some change has occurred which your son is upset about, and he is expressing his feelings in this way. If either you or his father is remarrying, breaking up with a dating partner, moving to a different place, or working longer hours, upset feelings can come out in disguised forms. If some fairly important life change has occurred, it could be helpful for you both to talk with him and be supportive of his feelings.

Neil Kalter

Q My two children, who live with their mother in another state, will be spending the summer with me. Do you have any suggestions to help them adjust and make our time together harmonious?

A Whether or not the noncustodial parent lives a long distance away, children of divorce who visit "the other home" have to be continually reacquainted with people, places and relationships. Dr. Clifford Sage's book *Treating the Remarried Family* (Bruner Mazel, 1983, $30.00) describes four phases of adjustment useful in dealing with children's visitation:

Preparatory Phase: About six weeks before the visit, both parents need to reassure their children that all plans for the visit are going to be carefully arranged. Discuss with your children the decisions being made and be sure to give them some power in the decisions.

Travel and visiting plans need to be carefully coordinated–paying attention to the details of traveling and routines and special requirements once they arrive.

When the child first arrives at the noncustodial home, it's more important to spend uninterrupted time together than to prepare elaborate activities. Preparing the child's favorite meal is a powerful "always welcome" message.

Transition Time (1 to 3 weeks): Frequent and scheduled telephone calls to "home" are important and need to be encouraged.

Behavior difficulties may begin to show themselves. Firm and consistent limits must be set down, and clear expectations by parents need to be spelled out. When your child says "My mom or dad does it differently at home," the noncustodial parent may say, "We do things differently here."

Middle Phase (bulk of the visit): Try to avoid packing a year's activities into a summer.

Keep visits with relatives short and reasonable – don't force the issue.

Respect your child's wishes about spending time in certain activities.

The biological noncustodial parent should try to be the disciplinarian so that the stepparent is less likely to be viewed as the "wicked one."

Leave-Taking Phase (the last 3 weeks): Telephone calls home need to be more frequent.

Specific traveling dates and details need to be taken care of.

Reassuring the children about continued contact with the "home" they are leaving needs to be communicated.

If attention to the above practical suggestions are heeded, harmony will certainly be enhanced over the summer.

Steven Spector

Resources:

❏ *At Daddy's on Saturday* by Linda W. Girard (Whitman, 1987, $11.25)

❏ *Helping Children of Divorce - A Handbook for Parents and Teachers* by Susan Arnsberg Diamond (Schocken Books, 1985, $11.95)

❏ *Mom's House, Dad's House* by I. Ricci (Macmillan, 1982, $6.95)

❏ *Quality Time - Easing the Children Through Divorce* by Melvin G. Goldzband (McGraw-Hill, 1985, $17.95)

❏ *Single Fathers* by Geoffrey L. Grief (Lexington Books, 1985, $8.95)

❏ *The Kid's Book of Divorce - By, For & About Kids* by The Unit at the Fayerweather Street School, Edited by Eric Rofes (Vintage Books, 1982, $3.95)

✔ Also see resources for preceding questions and under "Divorce" in *Contemporary Issues* section.

Q I'm 34 and single and thinking about marrying a divorced man with adolescent children.
What am I getting into?

A The marriage won't work if a man has to choose between his wife and children. Talk carefully with your potential spouse about what he expects your role with the children will be and what he sees as his role. Push for clarification.

Keep in mind that you can't compete with the mother of these adolescents and you don't want to. The important issue to consider is if you can "back off" and develop a friendship relationship with them; they need your support, not another mother.

One big problem with visitation is that expectations are set up on the part of kids that they will be entertained. If a new spouse has to give all of her time to amusing the kids, it's a dismal prospect for her and a poor idea all around. There must be interaction, but establish a schedule for each of you and stick to it.

Patricia Ryan

A What the children are probably feeling is some fear about being displaced since you have obviously gained a special place in their father's heart. Time and increased security can help diminish the children's natural defenses as they begin to feel safer inside a new family. Meanwhile expect that there will be times when all of you will feel confused and competitive with one another, and anxious about what to expect.

If possible gain an understanding from the children's natural mother of how she handles child-rearing issues. Agree ahead of time with the children's father about a consistent set of rules. When problems arise deal with them right away -- without overcompensating or overreacting. Be prepared to be tested, but also be prepared to be friendly.

Anne Soderman

Q I've been married for a year to a wonderful man with two children who live with us. Some days I don't think our marriage will survive, and most days I imagine the kids hope it won't. Please give us tips on how to live together peacefully.

A A stepfather or stepmother is frequently seen as an intruder when a parent with children remarries. The children often have not given up the fantasy that their parents will remarry. They view the stepparent in a blended family as the obstacle to the remarriage of their parents and are angry. They blame the stepparent and often show their anger in no uncertain terms. Their anger is transferred from their parents, whom they continue to love, to the stepparent. Their confusion is compounded because their parent remarried and they may believe he loves them less. These issues and others are very confusing to children and are often expressed in anger and oppositional behavior.

When parents and stepparents communicate openly, it is possible to resolve the issues. The children need to know that the noncustodial parent does not think that the stepparent is a "bad" person, that the stepparent did not cause the divorce, and that there is no chance for the parents to remarry. They need to hear that all the adults involved, care for them. A united front by the adults is very helpful. If the adults are in conflict, the children can play one off against another.

The children should be told no one is to be blamed for the divorce, certainly not the children. Children need to be reminded that parents are aware that divorce is painful for children and that they are still loved. Open communication is very important.

Many divorces are less than ideal and the original conflict between the adults continues with the children being used as pawns in the struggle. Then the stepparent has stepped on the proverbial hornet's nest. At times, the court must establish guidelines of behavior for the parents for the sake of the children. Counseling is often necessary and should include all parties involved, adults and children.

Joseph Fischoff

A **Every marriage experiences times when the spouses question its very survival.** We sometimes forget that marriages are like people and develop through stages including the good times and the bad. All marriages experience stresses and strains, a form of "marital aerobics" that can actually strengthen the intimacy within a relationship. New marriages, particularly those where children from prior marriages are involved, must struggle to establish a new system of relating.

The following hints may be helpful:

Marriages are for husbands and wives. Children benefit from the loving and intimacy of the marriage, but we are wrong when we think that our children come first. Adults and children are equal in any loving family.

It is important not to try to solve all problems immediately. Sometimes just letting things go can be helpful, but you may want to write down your personal concerns and look for patterns so that you are dealing with real problems rather than the temporary protests and testing of limits.

Don't try to force issues in stepfamilies. Premature scheduling of family trips and trying to rush creation of a new family system only results in anger and fear.

Don't assume that all problems are due to the fact that there are stepchildren involved. All marriages have their difficulties, and we sometimes look for the easiest explanation. Remember that the problems that are happening between children and stepparents are the stimulus for the formation of a new and stronger family group.

You may want to schedule an entirely new activity for you, your husband and the children. Do something that none of you have ever done before in your prior relationships. This allows everyone to enter into activities from a new perspective, beginning again without the "used to do's."

Paul Pearsall

Resources

▲ **Step Family Association of America** publishes a list of books, articles and the "Stepfamily Bulletin." Will also assist in forming local chapters. 602 E. Joppa Road, Baltimore, MD 21204
Stepping Ahead Program, designed by Emily Visher, and support classes are available through Southeast Michigan Chapter of Step Family Association of America. Youth are welcomed. Cora S. Webb, president. (313) 642-8226 (24-hour message)

▲ **The University Center for Children and Families,** University of Michigan Consultations with stepfamilies. (313) 764-9466; 8-8 M & W; 8-5 T, Th & F

❑ *How to Win as a Stepfamily* by EmilyB. Visher and John S. Visher (Dembner, 1982, $13.95)

❑ *Making It As a Step Parent: New Roles, New Rules* by Claire Berman (Harper & Row, 1986, $6.95)

❑ *Our Family Got a Divorce* by Carolyn E. Phillips (Regal, 1987, $5.95)

❑ *Second Marriage: Make it Happy, Make it Last* by Richard B. Stuart and Barbara Jacobson (Norton, 1985, $15.95)

❑ *She's Not My Real Mother* by Judith Vigna (A. Whitman, 1980, $10.75)

❑ *Stepfamilies: New Patterns of Harmony* by Linda Craven (Messner, 1982, $4.95)

❑ *Step-Kids: A Survival Guide for Teenagers in Step-Families* by McClenahan and Getzoff (Walker, 1984, $13.95)

❑ **Strengthening Your Stepfamily** by Elizabeth Einstein and Linda Albert (American Guidance Service, 1982, $10.95)

❑ **The Step-Family:** *Living, Loving and Learning* by Elizabeth Einstein (Macmillan, 1982, $14.95)

✔ Also see "Divorce - Visitation" in *Contemporary Issues* section.

Contemporary Issues

Q I understand that the state has mandated that our children have AIDS education in school. What will be taught? Who is in charge of this education?

A Public Act 185, which mandated AIDS education in Michigan's public schools, was enacted by the Legislature in November 1987. Exactly what will be taught, and when, is determined by each local school district. To help with this decision, the state departments of Public Health and Education have provided curriculum guidelines. AIDS information is also being incorporated as part of a comprehensive school health education program called the Michigan Comprehensive Health Education Model.

The AIDS epidemic has profoundly affected our society and many of us are concerned about educating our children. Schools must help prepare young people to deal with this epidemic. Young people may need this information to protect themselves now – or in the future. Whether for themselves or to help others, they *do need* the basic information about AIDS. Anyone who plans a career in medicine, education, counseling, the clergy or almost every other field needs to understand how AIDS is spread and how it can be prevented

Even very young children need information on AIDS. Elementary and preschool teachers tell us that children are afraid of AIDS. These children don't understand what AIDS is or how it is spread, but they hear adults talking or get bits of information from television. AIDS has become the new "bogey man-under-the-bed" for some children. We have a responsibility to provide good factual information about AIDS to protect young people from AIDS and to help them deal with "AFRAIDS," the fear of this disease.

Schools offer only one component of an AIDS education program. Parents and clergy must take an active part in providing information. Talk to your children. Make sure they have the facts. Encourage them to come to you if they have any questions. Work with your religious or community groups to provide programs that help clarify these complicated issues. Support the programs in your schools that offer knowledge, teach responsible decision-making and build positive attitudes toward health in general. The real danger of the AIDS epidemic is fear and ignorance.

Donald B. Sweeney

[A] **AIDS is a sensitive issue which poses many concerns and questions to parents and teachers.** In the few short years since AIDS appeared in the United States, much progress has been made in the fight against this disease. AIDS is an avoidable but fatal infectious disease for which there is no cure. HIV (Human Immuno-deficiency Virus) infection and AIDS strike the most productive group in society — young people.

We can protect our children from the AIDS epidemic. Our weapon is education.

The Michigan Department of Education's expert team recently completed AIDS curricula for K - 6th grade. The 7 - 12th grade curricula are already in school districts. These curricula are part of the Michigan Comprehensive Health Education Model.

For example, AIDS will be taught to 10-year-olds as part of the blood unit where children discuss different body defenses against disease. A 14-year-old will have three periods in a science class. The lessons will cover basic AIDS information, definition of terms, distinction between the levels of HIV infection, differentiating between myths and fact, transmission, how AIDS can be prevented, and identifying important AIDS messages.

Well in advance of any instruction, your school district will send you a letter telling you when the AIDS information will be discussed in your children's class. You will be invited to school to review the age appropriate material that was developed for your child's grade level.

Joy Schumacher

Resources

☎ **AIDS Hotline,** operated by U.S. Puiblic Health Service
1-800-342-AIDS, anytime

☎ **National AIDS Information Clearing House**
Request packet of information and sample materials.
1-800-458-5231, 7am-9pm M-F

☎ **Wellness Networks, Inc.**
A Michigan AIDS Information and referral hotline.
1-800-872-2437, 9-9 M-F; 9-5, S-S

▲ **Michigan Dept. of Health, Special Office on AIDS Prevention**
Center for Health Promotion
3423 W. Logan, P.O. Box 30195, Lansing, MI 48909; (517) 335-8371

✎ **"How To Talk To Your Teens and Children About AIDS"** (Free)
The National PTA, 700 North Rush St., Chicago, IL 60611-2571
(312) 787-0977

■ **"You Can Do Something About AIDS"** (1988)
A Cooperative Public Service Project of the Book Publishing Industry
Stop Aids Project, 40 Plympton St., Boston, MA 02118
Free from your local bookstore.

■ *Talking With Your Child About AIDS* and *Teens and AIDS* (1988)
Network Publications, ETR Associates
P.O. Box 1830, Santa Cruz, CA 95061-1830
(50 for $11.00, 200 for $40.00, 500 for $90.00 and 1,000 for $150.00)
Also from same publisher: *Does AIDS Hurt?: Suggestions for Parents,
Teachers and Other Care Providers of Children to Age 10*
by Marcia Quackenbush and Sylvia Villarreal (1988, $14.95)

❑ *AIDS: Facts and Issues* by Victor Gong and Norman Rudnick
(Rutgers University Press, 1987, $10.95)

❑ *Sex, Drugs and AIDS, a Book for Teens* by Oralee Wachter
(Bantam Books, 1987, $3.95)

❑ *The AIDS File* by George Jacobs and Joseph Kerrins M.D.
(Cromlech Books, Inc. Woods Hole, MA, 1987, $7.95)

❑ *Understanding AIDS* by Ethan A. Lerner, M.D., Ph.D.
(Lerner Publications Co., Minneapolis, MN, 1987, $9.95)

✔ Also see "Health Education" in *Home-School Connection.*

Q Drinking seems to be the main way for adults to celebrate the holidays. Often a family party ends in a fight because of drunkenness. My kids are watching. Our extended family is very important to us. What should I do?

A At holiday times people will occasionally abuse alcohol by drinking too much, too fast, in a misguided attempt to make the most of a special occasion. If your party includes alcoholics whose drinking is totally out of control, they will disrupt social affairs. These people need intervention and treatment. Intervention is a professional process by which a counselor can help family members and other caring persons to get their loved one into treatment.

In some cases, various ethnic traditions have raised holiday entertaining to such a high art that people look forward to parties not for the drinking, but for the puddings, cookies, pastries, breads and meats. One woman I know makes a pastry called Kristiania Kringle that is so good, it will bring tears to the eyes of a grown man! My own contribution is homemade pickled herring after my mother's recipe.

This strategy may take weeks of preparation and planning. Recruit others to share the work. When you succeed in presenting party fare so mouth-watering that people cannot stop eating long enough to get drunk, you will have put yourself in control. You will have also created warm memories for an entire extended family. What a gift that will be!

Of course, any alcoholic spirits served should be in the form of carefully diluted mixed drinks. Soft drinks should be available and non-alcoholic punches should be creatively prepared and abundantly present.

If this doesn't work, then we are back to the first consideration: Treatment planning, not party planning.

Dennis Nordmoe

A While we all feel obligated to invite family members to holiday gatherings, we need to reconsider our options when anticipating problems. You have a right and a responsibility to protect your children and yourself. If a particular extended family member's drinking creates problems, structure gatherings differently this year. Discuss your concerns with family members and use their support to replan. Here are some ideas:

Limit gatherings to your nuclear family.

Don't invite the problem drinker until you or your family can obtain professional help and intervene.

Don't serve alcohol. Focus on non-alcoholic drinks.

If you serve alcohol, choose low-alcohol products, limit varieties, and serve hearty foods.

Hold a separate "party" for children before or during the adult gathering.

Have shorter gatherings and specify starting and ending times.

Hold an early brunch or have dinner in a restaurant.

Leave early if visiting. While these alternatives may seem difficult, they are better than a family "fight."

Above all, talk to your children and communicate clear values about drinking. Provide an explanation of the physical, social and emotional consequences of drinking. If children observe drunkenness or fighting, talk with them and help them understand what happened.

If there is a problem drinker in your family, don't cover up drinking problems. It's important for children to see you not helping the person to drink. At the same time, you should treat the problem drinker with respect (he/she may have the disease – alcoholism).

Ilona Milke

■ **"The Great Pretender's Party Guide"**
from the American Automobile Association
(Free at AAA Michigan branch offices.)

❏ *Low Alcohol and Nonalcoholic Drinks*
(H. P. Books, P.O. Box 5367, Tucson, AZ 85704 , $9.95)
(602) 888-2150

❏ *Intervention: How to Help People Who Don't Want Help*
by Vernon Johnson (Moving Books,1988, $7.95)
P.O. Box 20037, Seattle, WA 98102

❏ *From Despair to Decision* by Louis B. Krupnik (CompCare, 1985, $6.95)
2415 Annapolis Lane, Minneapolis, MN 55441
Also available from Maplegrove Bookstore, Henry Ford Medical Center
6773 W. Maple, West Bloomfield, MI 48033
ED Note: Maplegrove carries many titles related to substance abuse.

Q In conjunction with spring parties and proms, the kids in this area are hiring limos and renting hotel/motel rooms to celebrate. The celebrating involves liquor, which is carried into the hotel or ordered from room service, and pot. The kids are all under the legal drinking age, and marijuana is illegal. As parents, we are under heavy pressure to let our youngsters attend. What's the hotel's/motel's responsibility in this?

A Parents have powerful allies in the law for that "rite of passage," the graduation party. Hotels and motels are liable (can be sued) on three fronts. A call from you will let innkeepers and others know that if anything goes wrong, the parent will be looking to the hotel/motel/limo owner for answers.

1. Laws, including the Dram Shop Act, have greatly expanded the legal responsibility of hotels and other public places to provide a "safe environment." The hotel must investigate if they have the slightest suspicion that teens are drinking on the premises. The hotel can be held liable for any accident, even one occurring hours after the party.

2. If a store or hotel sells liquor to a person under 21, the seller can be sued and lose his liquor license. This license means "big bucks" to those serving the public.

3. If minors are permitted to violate state or local ordinances, such as smoking pot and drinking, owners of hotels will be subject to criminal complaints, for example, contributing to the delinquency of a minor. Again, the liquor license can be taken away.

Melvin Guyer

A Although there are laws that hold hotels accountable in their business activities, parental responsibility is also an issue here. Parents, not hotels, are charged with the primary responsibility for the control and supervision of their children.

Children are always testing their parents. It is a part of the maturing process. Parents perceive this as pressure. Sometimes, in an effort to be a friend and/or maintain family tranquility, parents submit to the demands of their children even though they question the wisdom of their decisions. I understand parents register for rooms for their minor children. It's not fair or realistic for parents to expect others, i.e. hotels, to assume the role they have given up. Chaperoning continues to be appropriate where minors are involved.

Y. Gladys Barsamian

A Under Michigan law, organizations licensed to sell liquor must not furnish liquor to individuals under 21, or otherwise allow illegal use or possession on the premises. This means the bar, the restaurant, public areas or private rooms in a hotel. Staff are obligated to verify the age of anyone buying or receiving alcohol and refuse to serve alcohol if doubt exists.

Staff must also stop any illegal act in the hotel including the use of illicit drugs, such as pot, if they have seen the act, or if they are notified about it by other guests or staff.

Violation of the liquor laws can result in one or both of the following: fines or liquor license suspension by the Liquor Control Commission; or civil suit if someone is injured as a result of an illegal alcohol sale. For further information, contact Mr. Randy Martin, Deputy Director of Enforcement, Michigan Liquor Control Commission, (517) 322-1370.

Ilona Milke

Resources

▲ **Mothers Against Drunk Driving (MADD)**
Midland, MI 48641-2238
(517) 631-MADD

▲ **Project Graduation** prevents the adverse consequences of teenage alcohol and drug abuse through workshops, rallies and media publicity, state-wide.
Call Agnes Scott (313) 873-7200.

▲ **Students Against Drunk Driving (SADD)** work to: eliminate drunk drivers, alert students to the danger of driving drunk, conduct community alcohol awareness programs and organize peer counseling programs to help students who have concerns about alcohol. SADD offers a $35 starter kit to schools wishing to begin a new chapter.
P.O. Box 1073, Mt. Clemens, MI 48046
(313) 286-8800 Ext. 243

✎ *Michigan Parent Group Handbook: Preventing Teenage Drinking and Other Drug Problems* includes ideas from parent groups, listings of programs, workshops, speakers, research.
Michigan Substance Abuse & Traffic Information Center
925 E. Kalamazoo St., Lansing, MI 48912
(517) 482-9902

■ **"Be Party Smart"** a guide for teens (Free)
AAA Michigan, Safety and Traffic
One Auto Club Drive, Dearborn, MI 48126
(313) 336-1410

■ **Michigan Office of Highway Safety Planning**
Offers alcohol awareness information and programs for teens.
300 S. Washington Square, Suite 300, Lansing, MI 48913
(517) 334-7900

Q Several of my children's friends appear to be living with an alcoholic parent. How can I prevent my children from being exposed to alcoholism without cutting off their friendship?

A Another way to look at this situation is that you can "be there" for the children being raised in alcoholic homes. Be open and caring, and welcome the children to your home. Research shows that one strong, caring adult in the life of a child can make a difference between success and failure for that youngster.

According to the National Association for Children of Alcoholics, about seven million American youths under age 18 are children of alcoholics – four to six students per 25-member classroom.

Besides the pain of living with substance abusers, they face increased risks of physical and emotional abuse, becoming substance abusers, getting involved in abusive relationships, and having low self-esteem and high distrust.

To ease those difficulties, some schools offer counseling groups in which students learn they aren't responsible for their parents' substance abuse. Students identify problems in their own behavior and in relationships, and they learn solutions.

Check with your school's counseling or student assistance offices to see what services they provide and if a support group could be started. The resources which follow will be helpful to anyone raising or working with a child of an alcoholic.

Louise Reid Ritchie

☎ **Michigan Association for Children of Alcoholism and Other Addictions**
(313) 646-7010, 24-hour Hot-Line

☎ **Tel-Awareness** program provides free taped information 24 hours a day. Call **1- 800-227-7209** to hear tapes.
(Tape 133 describes Alateen support groups for children of alcoholics. Tape 314 describes how alcoholism affects families.) If calling from outside Michigan, dial (313) 227-7209. There are 50 taped messages. You must have a touch-tone phone. For a list of numbered messages, write or call Brighton Hospital, 12851 E. Grand River, Brighton, MI 48116 (312) 217-1211
ED NOTE: Tel-Awareness is a joint project of Brighton Hospital and **Michigan Communities in Action for Drug Free Youth.** *Call or write for free information regarding forming parent groups.*
470 N. Woodward, Birmingham, MI 48011; (313) 642-6270

▲ **National Committee for Prevention of Child Abuse**
Offers a Spider Man comic book about children of alcoholics, with tips on what to do about verbal abuse. ($2.00)
P.O. Box 94283, Chicago, IL 60690

▲ **Children of Alcoholics Foundation**
Publications for children of alcoholics including an excellent booklet, **"When Parents Drink Too Much."** ($1.50)
Write for list of audio-visuals and publications. P.O. Box 4185, Grand Central Station, New York, NY 10163; (212) 351-2680

▲ **Al-Anon** has information about free support groups for loved ones of alcoholics, including groups for children of alcoholics.
☎1-800-356-9996, anytime
P.O. Box 182 Madison Square St., New York, NY 10159-0182

▲ **Nar-Anon** support groups for families of drug abusers are active in some areas. Call (213) 771-9007 anytime for recorded information or write:
P.O. Box 2562, Palos Verdes Peninsula, CA, 90274

✔ **National Association of Children of Alcoholics**
Offers *Children of Alcoholics: Meeting the Needs of Young COA in the School Setting* by E. Morehouse and C. Scola (Single copies of this guide for starting a school program are $5.00 for non-members, $4.50 for members.) List of other materials mailed on request.
31582 Coast Highway, Suite B, South Laguna, CA 92677

❑ **Becoming Your Own Parent:** *The Solution for Adult Children of Alcoholics and Other Dysfunctional Families* by Dennis Wholey
(Doubleday, 1988, $17.95)
Features a number of founding members of the National Association for Children of Alcoholics.

❑ **Breaking the Cycle of Addiction:** *A Parent's Guide to Raising Healthy Kids* by Patricia O'Gorman and Philip Diaz
(Health Communications, 1987, $8.95)

For children and young people:

❑ **Living With a Parent Who Drinks Too Much** by Judith Seixas
(Greenwillow Books, 1979, $11.88)
Also by Seixas: **Children of Alcoholism:** *A Survivor's Manual* ;
Alcohol: *What It Is, What It Does* for Children 3-8. (1977, $2.95 each)
All available from :
National Council on Alcoholism, 12 W. 21st St., New York, NY 10010
(212) 206-6770

❑ **My Dad Loves Me, My Dad Has a Disease** by Claudia Black
(MAC Publishing, 5005 E. 39th Avenue, Denver, CO 80207; 1979, $8.95)

❑ **My House Is Different** by Kathi DiGiovanni. (Hazelden, 1986, $2.50)

❑ **Pot:** *What it is, What it Does* by Ann Tobias
(Greenwillow Books, 1979, $2.95)

❑ **Sometimes My Mom Drinks Too Much** by Kevin Kenny and Helen Knoll
(Raintree, 1980, $14.65)

❑ **The Brown Bottle:** *A Fable for Children of All Ages*
(Hazeldon, 1983, $4.95)

❑ **Welcome Home** by Judith Jance. (Franklin Press, 1986, $3.50)

❑ **You Can Say No to a Drink or a Drug:** *What Every Kid Should Know*
by Susan Newman. (Putnam, 1986, $8.95)

Q **What should I do if I suspect a neighborhood child is being abused?**

A Unfortunately, child abuse is all too common. It cuts across race, economic status, ethnicity and communities. Asking authorities to investigate is a critical step in protecting children. Call your county's Protective Services anytime. If workers feel a child is being mistreated, they will work with family members to help them learn to take proper care of the child and discipline without hurting.

Most parents, even those who abuse, love their children and want to do a good job. Abusive parents may have been abused themselves and know of no other way to raise children. Whatever their problems, they need help and their children need to be protected.

People who have abused their children and want to stop, or those who fear they are becoming child abusers, can join Parents Anonymous. It's rare that someone involved in Parents Anonymous is currently abusive, because other parents in the group won't tolerate it. They feel if they are trying to change, others should be trying also. They are both supportive and confrontive to abusers. In P.A. groups, only first names are used. Meeting places are not publicized. No walk-ins are allowed. New members are referred by the state P.A. office. It someone is referred or ordered by the court, progress reports are not made.

If it looks like a child is in danger, the P.A. group encourages the parent to make a self-report (85% of the time this is done by the parent). If the parent refuses, a report is made by P.A. There are many (but not enough) P.A. groups in Michigan. Call 1-800-482-0747. Professionals willing to volunteer three hours a week are badly needed as sponsors for P.A. groups.

Patricia Ryan

A Usually parents who have abusive tendencies toward their children have many problems – financial, marital or a whole range of problems. The family may feel isolated. Often a family will hide this very serious problem because parents are afraid or confused and not sure to whom to turn. Parents who abuse their children are not monsters. They are human beings who experience pain and anguish over their problem.

If you want to help this family, call Protective Services, listed in your telephone book under the Department of Social Services in your county. In an emergency, call the Sheriff's Department.

You do not have to identify yourself. Protective Services does prefer to have your name to obtain further information from you that may help to determine if the child is being mistreated. If you are willing to state your name, the Child Protection Law assures you confidentiality. You should have the names of the parents and their correct address in filing a report of suspected abuse.

A worker trained in making family assessments for possible child abuse will visit the family. Perhaps the protective service worker will find that the child is not being abused by the parents, but there is a problem of a hyperactive or a self-destructive child. Perhaps the worker will find reason to suspect the child is being abused...perhaps not. Appropriate referrals for professional treatment for the family will be made.

Guadalupe Lara

■ **"Abused Children Are Helpless Unless You Help"** (Free)
Michigan Committee for the Prevention of Child Abuse
116 W. Ottawa, #600, Lansing, MI 48933

▲ **Parents Anonymous of Michigan**
1553 Woodward - Suite 845, Detroit, MI 48226
(313) 237-0943 or **1-800-482-0747**

■ **"Questions About Child Protective Services"**
A pamphlet from the Michigan Department of Social Services.
Inquire at your local county office for a free copy.

▲ **National Committee for Prevention of Child Abuse**
332 S. Michigan Avenue, Suite 950, Chicago, IL 60604-4357
offers the following booklets for $2.00: "Annie Overcomes Isolation,"
"Caring For Your Children," "Words Can Hurt," "I Hear You," "Making The
World Safe For Jeffrey," "My Brother Got Here Early," "The Disabled Child
and Child Abuse," "Who Stole Mrs. Wick's Self-Esteem?" and "You're Not
Alone." Also available: *Child Discipline: Guidelines for Parents* by Gary
May and *What Every Parent Should Know* by Gordon Thomas (1987,
$2.50 each); *Growth and Development Through Parenting* by Elizabeth
Elmer. (1986, $3.00). For children there is a special edition of **Spider Man**
comics ($2.00).

❑ *By Silence Betrayed: Sexual Abuse of Children in America*
by John Crewdson. (Little, Brown, 1988, $17.95)

❑ *Some Secrets Are For Sharing* by Randy Winston-Hiller
(Macmillan, 1986, $5.95)

❑ *The Sexual Abuse of Children*
by Jeffrey Haugaard and N. Dickon Reppucci
(Jossey Bass, 1988, $27.95)

❑ *The Silent Children: A Parent's Guide to the Prevention of Child Sexual
Abuse* by Linda T. Sanford. (McGraw-Hill, 1982, $7.95)

■ *To Combat and Prevent Child Abuse and Neglect* (FL 588, $1.00)
Public Affairs Pamphlets
381 Park Avenue South, New York, NY 10016-8884

❑ *When Someone Takes Care of You* by Kay Koulouras and Ginny McCaig
(1986, $6.50). To be read to children by parents.
K & M Resources, 24200 Lahser Road, Southfield, MI 48034

Q We both work outside the home and good child care is our No. 1 concern. Are there guidelines to help find child care and where can parents turn for help?

A There are guidelines. First, decide which type of child care you want and can afford.

A caregiver who comes in may be the most suitable child-care arrangement, but the most expensive. In screening prospective caregivers, insist on several references and speak with the previous employers.

You and your husband (or another concerned person) should interview applicants to **assess experience, understand discipline methods, ascertain coping skills** (of the caregiver who will work in daily isolation with young children) and **discuss use of television.**

In a family day-care home, a caregiver takes care of several children. Check the home carefully. It should be registered or licensed by the State of Michigan. Be in touch with parents who have had children there. Inquire about the home's policy relating to sick children. This small, natural grouping of children is often preferred.

A third choice is a child-care center. Parents may prefer a well-run center because of its developmental and educational focus. The center should be licensed and have sufficient adult supervision. The groups should not be too large. Look for a variety of toys and equipment both indoors and outside.

Whatever type of care you are considering, involve your children. Have them visit your choice with you. Observe your children with the primary caregiver before you make a decision. You and your children must feel comfortable with that person. Never choose a home or center that does not allow parents to visit at any time during operation.

For help finding child care, begin with relatives, friends, neighbors and co-workers. Ask about their child-care arrangements. Also contact the Child Care Coordinating Council (4Cs)in your county for referrals.

Dorothy Kispert

▲ **Michigan 4C (Community Coordinated Child Care) Association,** a network of 13 locally and state-funded offices, provides information on how to find licensed day-care homes or centers in your area.

☎ Detroit/Wayne County 4C - **(313) 579-2777**

☎ Flint/Genesee County 4C - **(313) 232-0145**

☎ Grand Traverse Area 4C - **(616) 922-1115**

☎ Gratiot County 4C (Child Advocacy Association) - **(517) 463-1422**

☎ Ingham County 4C (Office for Young Children) - **(517) 887-6996**

☎ Kalamazoo County 4C (Child Care Resource & Referral) - **(616) 349-3296**

☎ Kent County 4C - **(616) 451-8281**

☎ Macomb County 4C - **(313) 469-6430**

☎ Oakland County 4C - **(313) 858-5140**

☎ Ottawa County 4C - **(616) 396-8151**

☎ Regional Mid-Michigan 4C - **(517) 695-5080**

☎ Upper Peninsula 4C - **1-800-541-KIDS** or **(906) 228-3362**

☎ Washtenaw County 4C (Child Care Coordinating and Referral Service - **(313) 971-5460**

✔ Call the state association at **(517) 351-4171** if there is no agency in your area or if you have questions regarding statewide child-care issues.

Q **What qualities should we look for in a caregiver?**

A With children often being cared for 50 hours per week, it is essential that they have quality care. Unfortunately, there are not enough qualified child-care providers to meet the current demand.

Look for a caregiver who is knowledgeable and experienced in:

child development

health/nutrition

safety/first aid/CPR

child guidance techniques

Be sure the caregiver is able to relate positively to children, parents and co-workers. Your child's caregiver should be responsible and dependable, accepting of individual differences, have a professional commitment, be sensitive and responsive to the needs of others, adaptable and flexible, and open to new ideas and learning. Other desirable character traits are a sense of humor, willingness to accept a challenge, and creativity.

The caregiver should be nurturing, a good listener and communicator, and physically able to handle the task. It is also important that your caregiver have a positive self-concept and outlook on life. If this sounds like a big order, remember ...your children don't deserve anything less.

Marlynn Levin

DAY-CARE CENTER CHECKLIST

Questions to ask when looking at day-care centers:

License number and when it expires_____

References _____

Teacher information_____

Educational degrees _____

Years of experience _____

Director information _____

Educational degrees _____

Years of experience _____

Ratio of kids to teachers?_____

How long has the center been in operation? _____

Can parents observe?_____

Does the center have transportation? _____

Any special programs?_____

Any field trips?_____

What type of activities?_____

What happens if you're late picking up your child at the end of the day? _____

Is there a hot lunch program? _____ Any snacks? _____

Cost: per week _____   per month _____

Registration fees? _____

Any discount for enrolling more than one child from a single family? _____

What is your discipline philosophy?

_____

What activities are provided?_____

_____

From The Merrill-Palmer Institute for Family and Human Development
Wayne State University, Detroit

■ **State of Michigan Day-Care Licensing**
Department of Social Services
P.O. Box 30037, Lansing, MI 48909
(517) 373-8300

✎ **"How to Choose a Good Early Childhood Program."** (Free)
National Association for Education of Young Children
1834 Connecticut Ave. NW, Washington, D.C. 20009
(202) 232-8777

❑ *The Parents' Guide to Day Care* by JoAnn Miller and Susan Weissman
(Bantam Books, 1986, $8.95)

❑ *The Preschool Years:* Family Strategies that Work from Experts and
Parents by Ellen Galinsky and Judy David. (Times Books, $19.95, 1988)

✎ **"The Stress of Balancing Work and Family"** by Christiann Dean and
Robert J. Fetsch (#HDFS 27, 70¢) and
"Let's Talk About Child Care" by Polly Spedding (#HDFS-19, 30¢) from:
Cornell University Distribution Center
7 Research Park, Ithaca, NY 14850-1247

❑ *The Woman Who Works, The Parent Who Cares:* A Revolutionary
Program for Raising Your Child by Sirgay Sanger and John Kelly
(Little, Brown & Co., 1987, $17.95)

❑ *Working and Caring* by T. Barry Brazelton
(Addison-Wesley, 1985, $8.95 paperback)
Offers sensible solutions to ease the fears and guilt of working parents.

✔ Also see resources under "Working Parents" in *Parenting and Family Life.*

Q How can working parents be prepared for child-care emergencies. For example, what can I do when my child becomes sick in school?

A Start by planning for the unexpected. Striking a balance between responsibilities of home and work is one of the most difficult tasks facing a working parent. A child's illness while a parent or parents are at work is a very stressful event. Parents who develop backup plans for a child's illness greatly reduce their stress levels and minimize the disruption to family and work.

Anticipating most potential child-care snags will help you design the type of backup system that really works in an emergency. After identifying potential problems (child gets sick at school or day care; school has emergency closing; child loses key to the house, etc.), begin listing every possible back-up option.

Consider friends, relatives, babysitters, neighbors home during the day, child-care centers, etc. List by priority. Often nonworking and working parents have had success joining together to form networks. Don't overlook them! Learn that asking others for help or ideas can take just a moment but may lead to a new strategy for coping with the unexpected. In some instances, groups of parents have paid a retainer to a person who will fill in when a child becomes ill or other emergencies. Also, you may consider scheduling "crisis standby duty" with other parents to plan for the calls at work.

John Abbey

✔ Some day-care centers offer school-vacation and snow-day care on an on-call basis. A few hospitals are now offering day care for sick children. Your area might even be fortunate enough to have a drop-in babysitting center. Sitter services are also an option – check the yellow pages. Investigate these options long before you need them – you may have to register in advance.

Q I am a single parent earning an entry-level salary. I've had to put my 2-year-old child in a day-care center that I feel is sub-standard, but it's the best I can afford. I worry about her all day, and I know it affects my performance on the job. How do I work with my employer to get our company to start a child-care center?

A Your employer needs encouragement to understand your need for quality child care. He needs to understand that his employees need assistance in finding quality child care, paying for quality child care and doing an excellent job for him while keeping family life in perspective. This is all in his best interests. It's the "bottom line" concept.

Here are proven procedures:

Find out where your company stands financially and idea-wise on child care. Is a full program possible, or partial service? Be aware of company needs as well as parent needs.

Suggest that a strong, fair-minded organizer from the company supervise the project.

The company needs to organize a task force which includes top management.

It is especially important that a consultant be hired who specializes in work and family life, has a background in child development and research skills, and understands business. The consultant must be experienced in presenting all the options to obtaining quality child care. The use of the consultant is cost-effective for the company.

The consultant, skilled in survey research, will assess the child-care needs of parents in the company. Policy decisions must be based on accurate information.

Once decisions are made, it is important that the consultant assist in developing appropriate programs.

A program developed correctly increases productivity, employee morale and improves the employer's chances of recruiting employees and retaining them.

You can make a difference in children's lives by working constructively with your employer on child-care issues.

The project will take hard work, careful planning and committment. **Today's children – tomorrow's citizens – are worth that effort!**

Marlynn Levin

Resources

■ **"Michigan Employers' Guide to Child Care"** (1988, free)
House Republican Task Force on Child Care
State House of Representatives, State Captiol Bldg., Lansing, MI 48913
(517) 373-3920

■ **"Speaking With Your Employer About Child Care Assistance"**
(Free) Fact Sheet #9 from the Child Care Action Campaign
99 Hudson St., Room 1233, New York, NY 10013.

■ **"Twenty Facts on Women Workers"** (1988, free)
U.S. Dept. of Labor, Office of Secretary, Women's Bureau
200 Constitution Avenue,NW, Washington, DC 20210

❑ *Employer-Supported Child Care: Investing in Human Resources*
by Sandra Burud, Pamela R. Aschbacher and Jacquelyn McCroskey
(Auburn House Publishing Co., 14 Dedham St., Dover, MA 02030; 1984,
$15.00)

❑ *Strenghtening Families Through the Work Place* by Peter Coolsen
(National Committee for the Prevention of Child Abuse, 1986, $4.00)
382 S. Michigan Ave., Chicago, IL 60604-4357
(312) 663-3520

Q My child, who is 10 years old, stays home alone after school until I return from work at 6:00 p.m. We have no alternative. What can I do to feel more secure about his safety?

A "Latchkey kids" are a fact of modern-day life. Millions (5 million, nationally) of school-age children are home alone for several hours a day.

Government and industry *do* seem to be making some progress in the area of affordable child care and flexible working hours, but so far reality is far from the ideal.

The National PTA is actively involved in improving this situation. Your local PTA can establish block parent programs, after-school enrichment activities and use "group strength" to encourage employers to adopt policies to meet the needs of families. In the meantime,

The National PTA recommends that your child know:

- his or her full name, address and phone number, including area code.

- your full name, exact name of the place where you work, and your work phone number.

- emergency phone numbers.

- how to carry a key so it is out of sight.

- that he/she should avoid walking home alone or playing alone outside after school.

- how to answer the phone without letting the caller know the child is alone. For example: "My mother can't come to the phone now. May I take a message?"

- to call a check-in person (you, a relative or neighbor) at a given time each day to let that person know everything's OK.

- how to respond to a knock at the front door. Decide if you want the child to ignore it or to say, "I can't help you now," and then make sure your child understands what to do.

- what to do if the child misses the school bus.

- what to do if there's bad weather after school.

- how to get out of the house quickly in case of fire. This includes knowing not to report the fire from the home phone because getting out of the house is the first priority.

Patricia Peart

Resources

✎ *Latchkey Children: Young Children at Home Alone*
An easy-to-read brochure produced by the National PTA and National Crime Prevention Council. (Single copy free; 100 copies for $4.00)
National PTA, 700 Rush Street, Chicago, IL 60611

✎ *It's 3 O'Clock...and It's Time to Help Children on Their Own*
A booklet to help families plan wisely so kids' time alone at home will be spent more safely and usefully.
(Stock number: 411-13404. 65¢ each, minimum order 25.
Bulk rates available on request.)
National School Public Relations Association
1801 N. Moore St., Arlington, VA 22209; (713) 528-5840

■ **Boy Scouts, Girl Scouts and Camp Fire, Inc.**
Offer survival skill booklets and other materials. Contact your local office.

■ **PhoneFriend Starter Kit**
A step-by-step guide telling how to set up a hotline for latchkey kids.
PhoneFriend, Box 735, State College, PA 16801

✔ Also see "Street Smarts" in this section.

Q Is there any one good time, in terms of the children, to get a divorce? Our home is mired in bickering, fighting and anger. I've given up trying to make peace with my husband. The kids, 5 and 7, are fighting more often as well. I worry about leaving my husband because I know the children need a father.

A Divorce is hard for children of any age. The "best" time for a marriage to end is when it is clear that it is not working and cannot work. It's a difficult decision. There is no time in a youngster's life when this change is easier than others.

What is most important is that parents be aware of how children feel and what they understand about their parents' divorce. When parents know the worries their children have at each age, they can help them adjust.

Early elementary school youngsters have:

thoughts/worries about having caused the divorce by being "bad" or difficult kids.

upset feelings about their parents' anger toward each other.

concerns about where the parent who leaves will live and if he/she will be all right.

questions about when they will see the parent who moves away.

sad feelings about not having their family all together.

worries about "losing" the parent they live with when he/she begins to date.

Here are several steps parents can take to help their children adjust:

1. Explain that divorce is "grown-up business." Kids don't cause divorce; grown-ups make the decision.

2. Keep angry feelings in check when with the children. "Bad mouthing" an ex-spouse when he/she isn't around hurts the kids.

3. Develop a clear schedule of parent contacts. A calendar with different types of stickers to show when a child will be with each parent helps.

If your child loses interest in school or friends, appears sad or withdrawn, or becomes a behavior problem, talk to him/her about the above points. Should troubles continue for over six months, a mental health professional can be consulted.

Neil Kalter

[A] There are three important points to consider when thinking about the effect of divorce on children:

1. How the parents' fighting is influencing the children.

2. The age of the child.

3. Whether you can divorce without excessive bitterness and arrange for frequent contact for each child with both parents.

With regard to point one, studies show continual exposure of children to fighting is more harmful than the divorce.

As for the age of children when divorce is recommended, there really isn't a good time. For infants and toddlers, bonding, security and safety issues predominate. If the child has a close emotional bond with the mother and his security is carefully considered, the absence of a father to whom the child may not yet be closely bonded may not be that detrimental.

Preschoolers may respond with separation anxiety, clinging, refusal to go to school and regressing in areas such as speech and toileting.

School-age children may respond with depression, aggressive behavior, and poor school performance.

Teenagers, who are emotionally and cognitively more mature, are usually most strongly impacted by divorce; they may rebel more, attempt suicide, run away or develop psychosomatic symptoms. Boys usually respond with aggressive, or conduct-disordered behavior; girls with depression and anxious behavior.

With reference to point three, if you can divorce without bitterness and arrange for frequent visitation and involvement of both parents, your children will not suffer as much as if you continue to have a battling and embittered response to divorce. Considering everything, I'd divorce before the children are much older. Are you certain you have tried every avenue to resolve the conflict with your husband?

Arthur Robin

Resources

✔ Call your principal, or your local family service agency or crisis intervention agency for counseling contacts.

▲ **The University Center for Children and Families,** University of Michigan (313) 764-9466; 8-8 M & W; 8-5,Ts, Th & F

❑ *The Divorce Workbook: A Guide for Kids and Families*
by S. B. Ives, D. Fassler and M. Lash (Waterfront Books, 1985, $10.95)

❑ *Helping Children of Divorce: A Handbook for Parents and Teachers*
by Susan Arnsberg Diamond (Schocken Books, 1985, $11.95)

❑ *Quality Time: Easing Children Through Divorce*
by Melvin G. Goldzband (McGraw-Hill, 1985, $17.95)

❑ *Single Fathers* by Geoffrey Grief (Lexington Books,1985, $8.95)

❑ *Raising Sons: Practical Strategies for Single Mothers*
by Joann Ellison Rodgers and Michael Cataldo
(New American Library, 1984, $14.95)

❑ *The Kid's Book of Divorce* by the Unit at the Fayerweather Street School, edited by Eric Rofes (Greene, 1987, $9.95)

❑ *How to Single Parent* by Fitzhugh Dodson (Harper & Row, 1987, $15.45)

❑ *Surviving the Breakup: How Children and Parents Cope with Divorce* by Judith Wallerstein and Joan Kelly (Basic Books, 1982, $9.95)

Q I'm planning to divorce my husband. We have two young children. What can I expect will happen from a legal standpoint?

A Your first task is to hire a good divorce lawyer. Get recommendations from friends who have gone through a divorce. Also check with the lawyer referral service run by your local bar association. Ask if he or she is a member of the Family Law Section of the State Bar of Michigan.

Make sure you have a written fee agreement with the lawyer you hire. Most lawyers will require a retainer fee of $500 to $1,500 before starting a divorce case. Lawyers bill by the hour in divorce cases, although a few will charge a flat fee for the entire case.

A divorce case involving children will take at least six months to complete. Sometimes that wait is much longer. If custody, support, property or alimony are contested, or if you live in a large county with a crowded docket, the wait could be a year or more.

Soon after your case is filed, you will be contacted by an agency called the **Friend of the Court**. It was created to help the judge decide custody, visitation, child support and alimony. The Friend of the Court also collects, disburses and enforces child support and alimony.

An employee of the Friend of the Court may interview both parents and the children. Information also will be gathered through a questionnaire. A written recommendation will then be presented to the judge and the attorneys for both spouses. Usually the judge will follow the Friend of the Court recommendation on child-related issues. The Friend of the Court will not make a recommendation on property settlement issues. This is left to negotiation between the spouses and their attorneys.

Fewer than 2 percent of Michigan divorces cases go to trial. Child custody decisions are based on the "best interest of the child." Child support is based on a formula that considers the incomes of both parents. Property is often divided equally, but an even split in not required by law. Alimony is rare in Michigan. It is common only in long-term marriages and where one spouse earns substantially more than the other.

After the divorce, custody, visitation, support and alimony can be changed if circumstances change. The property settlement, however, cannot be modified.

Scott Bassett

Resources

▲ *Divorcing* by Melvin Belli & Mel Krantzler (St. Martin, 1988, $22.95)
   ED NOTE: A famous divorce lawyer and a well-known psychologist team up to discuss hiring a lawyer, child custody, property and pain.

▲ **Michigan Office of Child Support**
   Department of Social Sevices
   300 South Capital Avenue, Lansing, MI 48909

❏ *How to Collect Child Support* by Geraldine Jensen. (ACES,1988, $6.50)
   Available from:
   The Association for Children for Enforcement of Support, Inc. (ACES)
   1018 Jefferson Avenue, Toledo, OH 43624

✔ Also see resources listed under other "Divorce" questions in this section.

Q I am separating from my husband after 10 years. We have two daughters ages 2 and 6. What type of custody is best for our children? My husband is very definite in wanting joint custody, saying he feels his input and care is vital to the children's well-being. I don't want to feel married to this man for the next 12 to 16 years.

A There are two kinds of joint custody: joint legal custody and joint physical custody.

Joint legal custody usually means that both parents continue to have a voice in important child-rearing decisions such as religious training, education and medical care. This arrangement is becoming increasingly common in Michigan – in some counties more than 25 percent of divorcing couples choose it. It has no implications for how much time children actually spend with each parent; it only refers to joint input into major decisions affecting children.

Joint physical custody is quite different. The children live part of the time with each parent, two or three days with one parent and the rest of the week with the other parent or alternating living a full week in each parent's home. This type of joint custody requires much more cooperation and good-will between parents and psychological flexibility on the part of the children than joint legal custody.

Recent studies in California and Michigan have shown that the kind of custody arrangement, whether it is joint legal, joint physical, or one parent having sole custody, does not determine how children adjust to divorce. **Children's adjustment is related to the quality of the post-divorce relationship** between parents, **each parent's emotional and social adjustment** to the divorce, **the economic security** of each parent, and **the quality of the relationship** between each parent and the child.

Neil Kalter

A Continuing post-divorce differences between the parents are harmful to children. Joint custody, which gives parents equal decision-making rights, was advocated in the 1970s with the hope that there would be fewer struggles between the custodial and non-custodial parents, since one parent would not have more decision-making rights than the other. The hope was that there would be fewer adversarial confrontations leading to repeated appearances in court. Unfortunately, joint custody has not been the solution that those who proposed it hoped it would be.

Joint custody rarely helps resolve the so-called "bad divorce" post-divorce relationships. The interpersonal struggles that led to the divorce continue and tragically, the children are involved. Parents who have joint custody and are embattled are not going to agree on what is "reasonable."

When parents decide that divorce is the best solution in an unhappy marriage, they usually continue to be interested in what is best for their children. They negotiate issues related to their children and arrive at reasonable decisions or compromises. They do not personalize the issues which result in blame, anger, frustration and repeated appeals to the court. Children are not used as pawns to win victories over the ex-spouse.

Parents who are mature place their children's welfare above their own. This may cause parents some degree of discomfort, pain and frustration, but they do not continue to battle. Either sole or joint custody is a viable option for parents who put their children's welfare first.

Joseph Fischoff

Q Our separation is ending in divorce. We both want custody of our child. How can I prevent a hostile battle between us over custody? I've read where parents accuse each other of mistreating and neglecting the child to get custody. How can we avoid this?

A Custody of children is a very important decision. Parents can decide on custody arrangements by themselves or make it a legal issue. If custody is made a legal issue, the decision will be made by others, typically the court, with input from various experts.

Legal battles over custody are generally difficult and prolonged and can leave emotional scars which might influence parents and children for some time.

I strongly recommend that parents make vigorous and good faith efforts to decide for themselves about the best custodial arrangement for their children. Parents should consider custody arrangements as a way of ensuring that their children continue to have an ongoing relationship with both parents after the divorce. Assistance for parents who want to make their own custody decisions can be provided by divorce mediators. Their services are available through the Friend of the Court without fee or through private divorce mediators, who charge.

Parents should remember that when they make allegations concerning the other parent's treatment of the child, such assertions, if unfounded, can be detrimental to the child and the quality of his future relationship with both parents. It is important to remember that a child needs an ongoing relationship with both parents both before and after the divorce.

Melvin Guyer

A When the battle over the custody of a child becomes hostile and parents resort to unfair fighting, every family member loses.

If you suspect your partner may be planning to falsely accuse you of abusing or neglecting your child in an effort to get an edge on the custody battle, talk to your partner through a mediator, who may be a lawyer, therapist or a counselor.

If communication has completely broken down, you must protect yourself and your child from having to go through medical examinations, social-worker inquiries and police investigations.

Some parents keep a journal and document everything their child does when they are together. Others have a third person present when the child is with them. The documenting of all injuries to the child is tedious but necessary if you are dealing with an untruthful and unreasonable partner.

Guadalupe G. Lara

Resources

✔ Obtain a copy of the **Michigan Child Protection Law** from your local Michigan Department of Social Services (In Detroit call 256-9661.)

❑ *Quality Time: Easing the Children Through Divorce* by Melvin G. Goldzband (McGraw Hill, 1985, $17.95)

❑ *Mom's House, Dad's House* by J. Ricci (MacMillan, 1985, $11.95)

❑ *Sharing the Children: How to Resolve Custody Problems and Get on with Your Life* by Robert E. Adler. (Adler and Adler, 1988, $17.95)

❑ *Surviving the Breakup: How Children and Parents Cope With Divorce* by Judith Wallerstein and Joan Kelly. (Basic Books, 1982, $10.95)
ED NOTE: This book is a classic by one of the nation's outstanding researchers, Judith Wallerstein; poignant and beautifully written.

For Mothers:

❑ *Mothers and Divorce: Legal, Economic, and Social Dilemmas* by Terry Arendell (University of California Press, 1986, $19.95)

❑ *Mothers on Trial: The Battle for Children and Custody* by Phyllis Chesler (McGraw Hill, 1986, $22.95)

❏ *The Custody Handbook: A Woman's Guide to Custody Disputes*
(Women's Legal Defense Fund, 1984, $7.00)

For children:

❏ *Mr. Rogers Talks to Families about Divorce*
by Fred Rogers and Clare O'Brien. (Berkley Books, 1987, $6.95)
ED NOTE: Visit your local library to review books for children about divorce. Suggest to your child's school that they stock your recommended titles.

❏ *Why are We Getting a Divorce?* by Peter Mayle
(Harmony Books, 1988, $11.95). A book to help parents understand children's concerns and offers sympathy and reassurance to children.

For fathers:

■ *Fathers' Journal: The Monthly Publication of Fathers for Equal Rights of America*
Fathers For Equal Rights of America, Alan Z. Lebow, Exec. Director
P.O. Box 2272, Southfield, MI 48037
(313) 354-3080

■ **National Congress For Men**
3715 Brewerton Road, N. Syracuse, NY 13212
(315) 455-7043 or (315) 638-4216

❏ *Dimensions of Fatherhood*
edited by Shirley M. H. Hanson & Frederick W. Bozett
(Sage Publications, 1985, $16.95)

✔ Also see resources under other "Divorce" questions, this section and "Single Parenting" and "Stepparenting" in *Parenting and Family Life* section.

Q We are worried that our kids will get involved in drugs. Their school is putting on a big campaign about saying "no." What can we do besides just telling them to "say no"?

A Contributing positively to your child's self-esteem is the single most important step you can take to help him make the right decisions about drug and alcohol use. A teen's most vulnerable moment is when he is faced with peer pressure, rejection and/or failure. If a youngster feels good about himself and has good coping and problem-solving skills, the temptation to "go along with the crowd" in order to be accepted or to "ease the pain" with substances is greatly reduced.

Twenty years of dealing with drug issues has shown us that neither information, nor forbidding alone will keep your child from abusing drugs. Besides developing self-esteem and problem-solving skills, it is important to discuss drugs with your teen in a non-threatening atmosphere. Know the facts, listen attentively, and clearly express your attitudes, values and fears. Then pray.

Helene Mills

A We must be concerned about all children facing the pressure to use drugs. The most successful prevention programs help children and teens build self-confidence, social skills and coping skills. As a parent you can teach your child:

Honest communication. Children need to learn how to express their feelings, such as anger, joy, love and fear, and they need to believe it's safe and appropriate to do so. You also must learn to express your feelings honestly. Ask your children how they feel, especially if you know something is bothering them or if you have just scolded them. Be a good listener, and teach your children to listen.

Cooperation. Children must learn to cooperate, negotiate and put themselves in another's shoes so they can get along with others. Help them practice by negotiating what TV programs to watch or where to go on vacation. Praise your children for cooperating, especially when they don't get what they want. When they do get what they want, make sure they are considerate of those who did not.

Personal Responsibility. Teach your children to take responsibility at an early age and gradually increase their responsibilities to help them build a strong self-image. Give your children meaningful tasks that demand the use of their mental and physical abilities. Make sure they are capable of doing the tasks. Help and encourage them.

The Ability to Make Judgments and Decisions. This is a valuable tool in helping your children resist the crowd that offers them drugs. Children learn these skills by being with mature people who make judgments and decisions. Let your children practice making judgments and decisions often. Urge them to think of the various choices they have and the consequences of each.

National PTA

Resources

✔ **Drug and Alcohol Prevention Project of the National PTA** provides information for leaders on planning and implementing prevention projects.
National PTA, 700 Rush Street, Chicago, IL 60611-2571
(312) 878-0977

▲ **American Council for Drug Education**
204 Monroe St., Suite 110, Rockville, MD 20850
(301) 294-0600, 9-5 M-F

▲ **The Paper People** is a school-based substance abuse prevention program for children and their parents in the primary grades.
8 sessions, training, materials, program.
The Knopf Co., 1126 S. Main St., Plymouth MI 48170
(313) 455-4343

■ **Brighton Hospital** offers free booklets on substance abuse: **"Alcohol and the Family," "Cocaine and the Family"** and **"Marijuana: A Second Look."**
12851 E. Grand River, Brighton, MI 48116
(313) 227-1211, 8:30 - 4:30 M-F

■ **Community Intervention, Inc.**
offers the following booklets for $2.95 each (shipping included):
"Athletes and Drugs: A No-Win Combination," "Adolescent Drug and Alcohol Use," "Crack: The Rock of Death," "Saying Yes, Saying No."
529 S. Seventh St., Suite 570, Minneapolis, MN 55415
1-800-328-0417

■ **National Clearinghouse for Alcohol and Drug Information**
P.O. Box 2345, Rockville, MD 20852
(301) 468-2600, 9-5 weekdays

■ **"Children and Drugs"** (#FL584, $1.00)
Public Affairs Pamphlets
381 Park Avenue South
New York, NY 10016-8884

❑ **"What Works: Schools Without Drugs"** (U.S. Dept. of Education, free)
Schools Without Drugs, Pueblo, CO 81009
1-800-624-0100

✔ Also see resources under "Self-Esteem" in *Parenting and Family Life.*

Q I've heard that in some areas youngsters are selling bags of crack on the street for $3.00. But we live in a good neighborhood and I'm not aware of any drug problems at the grade-school level. Do I need to be talking to my 7-year-old son about drug abuse this soon?

A Because children from all neighborhoods may be tempted to use tobacco, drugs and alcohol, your question is important for all families, whether or not they live where obvious drug-dealing occurs.

Studies have indicated that by the time children are 9 years old they have formed values about substance abuse. So start educating your youngsters about drugs, alcohol and tobacco as soon as they can talk.

Begin by informing them that tobacco, alcohol and medications can be poisonous. By the time your youngsters are in kindergarten, discuss other consequences of substance abuse. Concentrate on aspects that would be meaningful to children such as bad breath and stained teeth from tobacco use, queasiness from alcohol use, and peculiar behavior that can result from drug use. Point out tobacco and liquor advertisements and talk about false messages they may contain.

Because learning specifics about how street drugs are used tempts some youngsters to experiment, don't give that kind of information. Most importantly, since children learn best by your actions rather than your words, don't use tobacco or street drugs and avoid irresponsible alcohol and prescription drug use.

Louise Reid Ritchie

A As early as fourth grade, your children may know something of the drug scene, says the National Institute on Drug Abuse. Parents can do something about it, says the National PTA.

Why do young people use alcohol and other drugs? The reasons are complex and varied. Your challenge as a parent, however, is to try to keep your children from using drugs in the first place. You have a lot more power to prevent your children's future use and abuse of drugs than you may think. The time to begin is now.

Teach your children to feel good about themselves. Teach them to be able to give and receive unconditional love. Love your children for who they are regardless of what they achieve or how they perform. Even if they anger you, let them know that you still love and respect them as persons.

Give your children a positive role model. Your children will feel good about themselves if you feel good about yourself. Positive role models will help your children gain healthy habits and attitudes. The examples you set also will help your children resist pressures to use alcohol and other drugs – pressures they receive from movies, television shows and commercials, and perhaps from their friends.

National PTA

Resources

❑ *Crack: What You Should Know About the Cocaine Epidemic* by Calvin Chatlos, M.D. (Perigee Books, 1987, $5.95)

❑ *Drug Abuse and Your Teens: What Every Parent Should Know.* (National Communication, Inc., 1983, $6.95)

❑ *Growing Up Free* by Letty Cottin Pogrebin (Bantam Books,1980, $8.95)

❑ *It's O.K. to Say No to Drugs* by Alan Garner (RGA Publishing Group Inc., $9.95)

❑ *Kids and Drugs: A Parent's Guide - How to Tell if Your Child is Using Drugs and What to Do* by Otteson, Townsend and Rumsey (CFS Publishers, 1983, $8.95)

❑ *Loosening the Grip:* A *Handbook of Alcohol Information* (Mosby, 1982, $17.95)

❑ *Marijuana:* Its *Effects on Mind and Body* by Marion Cohen (Chelsea House, 1985, $17.95)

❑ *A Parent's Survival Guide* by Harriet Hodgson (Harper/Hazelden, 1986, $6.95)

❑ *Setting Limits: Parents, Kids and Drugs* by William LaFountain (Hazelden, 1982, $1.75)

❑ *Steering Clear* by Dorothy Cretcher (Winston Press, 1982, $4.95)

❑ *You Can Say No to a Drink or a Drug:* What *Every Kid Should Know* by Susan Newman (Perigee, 1986, $8.95). *ED Note: Stories about drinking and marijuana. Photos of kids partying, drinking, making decisions. Excellent for late elementary and junior high.*

❑ *The Parent Connection:* How to *Talk to Your Child About Alcohol and Other Drugs* by Roberta Meyer (Franklin Watts Publishing, 1984, $14.95)

❑ *What to Believe About Drugs* An *Honest and Unhysterical Guide for Teens* (Holt, 1987, $12.95)

Q Our daughter has been diagnosed as having anorexia nervosa and bulimia. We don't understand these diseases. How can we help her recover?

A Anorexia nervosa is a life-threatening disease involving self-induced starvation, compulsive dieting, serious weight loss, unrealistic fear of eating and weight gain, and refusal to maintain a normal body weight.

Anorexia often develops during adolescence, is more common in girls than boys, and if untreated, results in serious medical and psychological consequences, including the possibility of death. We do not know for sure what causes anorexia nervosa, but we believe that cultural pressures for thinness, heredity, stresses within the individual and stresses from the family all contribute.

Girls do not usually recognize that they are becoming anorexic. Parents and teachers need to be on the lookout for the following kinds of danger signs:

Serious weight loss for 3-6 months.

Period stopping for several months (not due to pregnancy).

Unusual dieting or changes in eating which restrict many types of food.

Fears of getting too fat or eating.

Unusual increase in exercising.

Eating large amounts of food or vomiting after meals.

It is much easier to reverse anorexia if we catch it early. Parents who see these signs in their teenage daughters should seek professional help.

Arthur Robin

A Bulimia includes fear of overeating followed by self-induced vomiting or use of laxatives or diuretics. It is a life-threatening disease that greatly interferes with emotional and psychological growth and development. Unlike the anorexic, a bulimic may appear perfectly normal, causing the disease to go undetected for a longer time.

A young woman who has developed bulimia is feeling a great deal of stress and usually sends out signals or a disguised cry for help. I strongly urge parents to watch for these signals and not be convinced by anyone that self-induced vomiting, or the abuse of laxatives or diuretics is "just a part of growing up," or a safe way to control weight.

Only your daughter can take responsibility for change. However, parents who educate themselves and become involved in treatment can be tremendously helpful.

Perhaps the single most important thing you can do now is to tell her you are concerned because you care and you want to help.

Do not focus on food; remember, this is a problem of feelings, insecurities, self-doubt and low self-esteem.

Do not allow yourself to feel guilty.

Continue to ask questions, gain understanding of feelings, conflicts and stress.

Seek professional help as soon as possible.

Ann Weeks Moye

Resources

▲ **American Anorexia/Bulimia Association**
Dept. P., 133 Cedar Lane, Teaneck, NJ 07766
(201) 836-1800, 9:30-5:30 M-F; 6:30-8:30 Th.

▲ **National Anorexic Aid Society**
5796 Karl Road, Columbus, OH 43229
(614) 436-1112, 9-8 M,Th; 9-4 F

▲ **Eating Disorders Support Groups** for anorexic and bulimic persons and their families and friends. Several groups meet at various locations throughout the state.
William Beaumont Hospital, Royal Oak
Dr. Alexander Sackeyfio
(313) 471-0785.

■ **Anorexia/Bulimia Program at Children's Hospital of Michigan,** Detroit
Dr. Arthur Robin
(313) 745-4878 (8:30-4:30)

☎ **Eating Disorders Hotline**
(614) 436-1112 or **(313) 973-9700**; 8-8, M-Th; 8-5, Fri.

☎ **Anorexia Nervosa and Related Eating Disorders Inc.**
P.O. Box 5102, Eugene, OR 97405
(503) 344-1144; 24-hour hotline

❑ *The Golden Cage: The Enigma of Anorexia Nervosa* by H. Bruch
(Random House, 1985, $3.95)

❑ *When Will We Laugh Again: Living and Dealing With Anorexia and Bulimia* by Barbara Kinoy and Estelle Miller
(Columbia University Press, 1983, $14.00)

❑ *The Best Little Girl in the World* by Steven Levenkron
(Warner, 1979, $3.95)

❑ *Breaking Free From Compulsive Eating* by Geneen Roth
(NAL Penguin Inc., 1986, $3.95)

❑ *Feeding the Hungry Heart* by Geneen Roth
(NAL Penguin Inc., 1983, $3.95)

❑ *My Name is Carolyn* by Carolyn Miller (Doubleday, 1988, $16.95)

❑ *Surviving an Eating Disorder, New Perspectives and Strategies for Family and Friends* by Michele Siegel, Judith Brisman, Margot Weinshel
(Harper & Row, 1988, $15.95)

Q I know that TV can and does teach values to my children. What kind of values does it teach, and whose values are they? I definitely don't want my kids to grow up to be like J.R. on "Dallas."

A If we don't want the values of television drama to become the values of our children, then we must teach our children what we believe to be right and wrong, good and bad. Children are powerful little learning machines, running around in the world paying attention to everything. Whatever they are exposed to they learn about.

Television is part of their world, and television provides endless amounts of information – not all of it good or complete. Television is never too tired or too shy to say what it believes. What about parents? Do they speak up for what they believe and care about? Do they realize how many other voices their children hear? I wonder.

Let me give you an example. Children are exposed to about 30,000 television commercials a year, half of which are for food. Candy and sugared cereal are a large part of the food that is advertised to children, and dental authorities believe that this kind of food is the cause of tooth decay and cavities.

So let's say that children are exposed to about 10,000 messages a year telling them to eat heavily sugared food. How many times a year do parents remind these same children that it is important to brush their teeth after eating? I can tell you how many times television tells them this – none. So if children are going to learn this important health information, parents need to provide it.

Parents are up against the same influence from television in the moral arena. On television thousands of characters cheat and lie and few are honest.

If we want our children to value what we value, we must teach them what we believe. A good time to do this is while watching television. Right in the middle of the program you could say, "I don't want to be like J.R. I don't like that kind of person. What J.R. does to people is wrong..." When we do this, we give our children a choice, and we tell them which end of the choice we would make. We have to leave the rest to their good sense.

John Condry

A Children learn a tremendous amount from TV; how to act, think and feel. Values on TV can become your child's values. Many of the family situation comedies project positive values. However, the majority of TV programs present values you and I might consider negative or unhealthy.

TV program scripts are not written with the intention of corrupting the morals of our youth, but to entertain. TV entertains by reflecting a segment of the population, how they feel, act and what they value.

Be careful of the types of programs your child watches. TV is presenting our children with a set of values very different from those of past generations. Most of the negative values on TV can be listed under one of the following:

Anti-personal relations values. Human life is not valued. Murder is often presented as the only alternative. Victims are not seen as humans with feelings. People just become props for the story line.

Anti-cooperation values. No need for mediation, compromise or attempts to work problems out. Everything is a conflict. People work as a loner solving their own problems by violence. Conflicts that could be solved with conversations are solved with action – all within 30 minutes.

Anti-democratic values. Law are written for other people. It's OK to break the law as long as your intentions are good. The government, police and other law agencies are portrayed as the enemy, or uncaring or incompetent.

Anti-family values. Families are not important, nor are they portrayed as strong pillars of society, a place with trusted family members where children can turn for help and advice.

When children watch programs with negative values the TV values will become their values, unless parents take a more active role in monitoring TV viewing, being forceful in modeling their own family standards and ideals, and talking with youngsters about the images and values projected on TV.

Marilyn Droz

Resources

▲ **Council for Children's Television and the Media**
Has guidelines for a school program which helps children view TV critically and develop their own values. A parent's handbook, filled with practical suggestions, is also available.
33290 W. 14 Mile Rd., West Bloomfield, MI 48322
(313) 489-5499

❑ *Getting the Most Out of TV* by Dorothy G. Singer
(Scott Foresman, 1981, $10.95)

✎ *"Parents, Children and TV"* by Dorothy G. Singer and Helen B. Kelly
(The National PTA , $1.00)
National PTA, 700 N. Rush Street, Chicago, IL 60611

■ *Parents' Choice*
A newspaper with reviews of children's books, TV programming, movies, recordings, toys, games and computer programs. ($22.00 for 8 issues)
Parents' Choice, Box 185, Newton, MA 02168
(617) 965-5913

✔ Also see resources under "Alternatives to TV" in *Parenting and Family Life.*

Q We now have cable TV available in our area. How does cable differ from regular TV? Is it worth getting for family viewing?

A Families can usually find something worth watching together on a cable TV system. Most cable systems include "Nickelodeon," a channel for youngsters, in the basic fee and offer "The Disney Channel" as a premium.

Cable TV reaches us by a cable that is hung between telephone poles or buried underground and then connected to your TV. It is in a little more than half the homes in this country. Large cities have been slow in allowing cable companies to begin.

There are more than 60 cable television networks that send their programs to satellites. In cities where there is a cable business, that business chooses which networks it wants to have on its system. It receives the television program from the satellite on its dish, and sends the program along the cable to homes of subscribers.

Most cable systems carry 30 to 36 channels, compared to the four or five without cable. Most carry commercial television networks, super-stations (New York, Atlanta, etc.) a public television channel, an all-sports channel, an all-news channel, a weather channel, a music channel, several channels that carry messages of local school events, city government, etc.

Cable systems also carry "pay" or "premium" channels (you pay extra). Most of the pay channels carry movies with no advertising. Cable television costs about $16.00 per month. Pay channels cost about $8.00 extra, with a discount for buying several channels.

Bradley S. Greenberg

A The average cable viewer watches an extra 7 hours of TV a week, according to Nielsen surveys. This additional TV viewing can have a negative effect on families and children. Despite the variety, after a few weeks most people limit their choices to just a few channels.

In cable homes parents may have less control over their children's viewing. Here are guidelines from "The Cable Connection," a booklet from the Council for Children's Television and the Media:

Never watch cable without checking in a TV guide to see what your choices are. Don't rent a remote control; this encourages TV scanning, rather than responsible choosing.

Ask the cable company for a free parental code lock, and lock out programs you feel are not appropriate for your children, such as MTV.

Don't always watch the same programs every week. Try new programs.

Don't let TV use up all your leisure time.

Evaluate the cost of premium channels against the cost of renting tapes, going to sporting events, your county park system or museums. Folks who have the movie channel tend to watch it just because it's paid for.

Establish TV viewing rules, and see that they are enforced.

Cable can offer your family a rich variety of programs that will improve your viewing, or it can bring into your home violence, sex and poor values. The choice is yours.

Marilyn Droz

Resources

❑ *Cable and Children: An Action for Children's TV (ACT) Handbook* Available for $3.50 from ACT, 20 University Road, Cambridge, MA 02138.

❑ *Unplugging the Plug-In Drug* by Marie Winn (Viking, 1987, $18.95)

✔ Also see resources under "Media Influence."

Q What effect will "pop rock" and MTV have on my child who is 11. He loves to listen and wants to go to concerts featuring rock stars. I can't even understand the words being sung. What should I do?

A Music has always been a traditional way for children to express their individuality and help with their separation from adults. It plays a major role not only in value development but also in socialization.

Pop rock means popular rock – it's the rock you hear on the radio and is not so blatantly suggestive as *Heavy Metal* and other types of rock – such as *Death Metal, Speed Metal* and *Hard Core Metal* which is the most radical.

Listen carefully to the music. Some songs of today are about the same things that lyrics have always been about. Others, however, are meant to shock and deal with subjects like incest, satanism, sadomasochism, bestiality, bondage, sexual violence, drugs, drinking, rebellion and suicide as problem-solving. The lyrics often condone these behaviors as acceptable.

Children rely heavily on music videos to interpret the music. Teens are influenced by their music even when they disagree with the lyrics. Music videos are based heavily on stereotyping and surrealistic fantasies. Thirty-nine percent of all violence on music videos is sexually related and 34 percent of sexual references are homosexual.

Watch the music videos your children enjoy. Use the music and the lyrics as an opportunity for dialogue. You'll hear the lyrics differently than your youngsters. Talk about the performers – and their role modeling.

Before you let your child go to a rock concert, find out:

What type of security is provided?

What is the age of the audience?

What were the reactions of previous crowds at other performances?

Is a medical team present?

Is drug use overlooked?

Will the promoters allow head banging (jerking heads in unity), **stage diving** (climbing on the stage and jumping off into the crowd) and **mashing** (violent bumping each other)?

You can find out the above by calling the stadium or club where the performance is held. Your family record store can help with information, too. Don't hesitate to go with your child. A rule of thumb is the smaller the place, the more radical the music.

What else can you do?

Ask your record store owner for the rating of the album. This will give you information as to how explicit the lyrics are.

Most records come with lyric sheets. Read them.

Listen to the words, not just the music.

Don't encourage your child to use a headphone – hear what he is hearing.

Talk about the messages of the song. Be sincere and interested – the conversation should be thoughtful.

Don't allow rock that is offensive to you in your home. In a relaxed, non-hostile way, tell your child why you find it offensive.

Point out that video offers only one interpretation of the song.

Influence your children's taste by introducing them, at an early age, to good popular music, jazz or classical music.

Watch for changes in your child's music taste.

Music can offer an opportunity for children to explore their values and beliefs, or it can be a destructive force. You can help decide what part music will play in your child's life.

Marilyn Droz

Resources

▲ **Council for Children's Television and the Media**
33290 W. 14 Mile Road, Suite 488, West Bloomfield, MI 48322
(313) 489-5499

▲ **Morality in Media,** 475 Riverside Dr., New York, NY 10115

▲ **National Coalition on Media Violence**
P.O. Box 2157 Champaign, IL 61820

▲ **Parents Music Resource Center;**1500 Arlington Blvd., Arlington, VA 22209

❏ *Getting Closer: Discovering and Understanding Your Child's Secret Feelings about Growing Up* by Ellen Rosenberg (Berkley Books, $7.95)

❏ *How to Live (Almost) Happily With a Teenager* by Lois and Joel Davitz (NAL,1983, $3.95)

❏ *Raising Positive Kids in a Negative World* by Zig Ziggler (Nelson, 1985, $14.95)

❏ *Why Knock Rock* by Dan and Steve Peters (Bethany House, 1984, $6.95)

Q What can parents do when their 16-year-old runs away from home? We have filed a police report and notified the school, but what else can we do?

A You have taken the most important steps. If the child reports to school personnel, they will notify you. Find out from your police precinct, who is the officer handling your child's case. Call this officer daily to request the status of your case. Make available pictures of your child to the police.

Next, contact your child's friends and notify their parents of your concern. Often a runaway child will stay over at a friend's home and tell the friends that they have permission from their parents.

Contact your local YMCA or Youth Center where young people congregate and inform them of the problem. Leave sealed notes for your child at these various places. This will let your child know he or she is missed and that you are willing to negotiate for his or her return.

Contact a runaway center and ask for a counselor who can mediate between the child and the parent. There are no perfect parents or perfect children, it is only through communication that we can reach an understanding.

Guadalupe Lara

A Once you have done all you can legally, ask yourself these questions:

What might your child be trying to run "to?" – not just what he is running "away from." Is he seeking something that you agree is lacking in your family? What could be done now to fill that gap and make the child's return possible?

Have you, too, felt like running away? If so, why? What are your personal stresses, disappointments and fears related to your family? Focusing on your own feelings may help you understand the feelings of the absent child, and make his or her return possible.

Remember that blame, guilt and self-recrimination will do nothing to bring your child back. Attempting, through professional help, to create a more positive family environment is more productive.

As strange as it may seem, try communicating with the absent child with your thoughts, prayers, even attempting to send mental messages. Whether or not you believe in this process, such positive thinking can help heal the broken family system.

Don't forget the other family members. Sometimes the pain of a runaway child distracts us from their needs. The absence of one family member should result in the unification of the remaining members. Professional counseling may be necessary.

Children run away for as many reasons as there are runaway children. To confront this issue, seek professional help, not just to discover why a child ran away, but to identify family strengths that can be mobilized.

Paul Pearsall

Q My daughter has just returned from running away for three days and I don't know how to handle it. On one hand I'm furious that she left, and on the other, I'm happy she's home. I'm afraid if I ground her she will just run again. What do I do?

A Adolescents often communicate with actions rather than words. It is important to understand your daughter's behavior before you take action. Running away could be a cry for help or an attempt to escape family problems. It could result from peer pressure or a need for independence. Youngsters at different ages run away for different reasons.

Punishing the behavior without handling what your daughter sees as a problem will not help. A family meeting to discuss feelings in the family and to negotiate more constructive ways of handling problems might be helpful. If this kind of listening and discussion is difficult for your family, do seek counseling.

Carol Mitchell

A Grounding her is not the answer. Unless there is listening and talking between you and your daughter, the running away may happen again. To begin, you need to clear the air, clarify what went on and why.

The running away can be a part of several other things: failing in school, anger – even temporary anger, drug use, following friends, being afraid. These are serious issues. Basic to all is that disciplining your daughter for running away may not help at all. You may want to call a private therapist or a family services agency in your area.

Joseph Fischoff

A The National Network of Runaway and Youth Services estimates that 1 in 10 children run away annually, totalling a force of 1.8 million children hitting the streets. Young people run away for all sorts of reasons, but the bottom line is a feeling of being unwanted or unloved at home. Striving for adulthood, testing limits, learning who they are and what their inner strengths are makes the teen years full of failures and great sensitivity. It is the period of greatest transition in life.

Young people need structure and freedom to grow, and the balance between them is difficult to achieve. Most of us make mistakes in learning how to strike this balance, and the highly sensitive, idealistic teen interprets any waivering as a personal affront. As parents, we must be very conscious of this transition, diligent in keeping the communication lines open and patient.

Chances are the frustration, anger or fear that drove your daughter from home is a feeling you're experiencing as well. Examine that possibility and share your feelings of fury, relief and uncertainty with your daughter. She needs to know how worried you were, that you love her, and that you're angry about her leaving. If you're not able to share these feelings without closing off two-way communication, contact one of the runaway programs throughout the state. These agencies are specifically designed to help you and your daughter work through problems. The Michigan Rapline (see below) will give you the number of the nearest program.

Meri K. Pohutsky

Resources:

☎ **Common Ground,** 751 Hendrie, Royal Oak, MI 48009
(313) 645-9676, 24-hours, face-to-face and telephone crisis intervention and referrals for metropolitan Detroit.

☎ **Crisis Telephone Service,** Midland (517) 631-4450, 24 hours.

☎ **Michigan RAP** (Runaway Assistance Program) 1-800-292-4517, 24 hours.
Telephone counseling for runaways and their parents.
Referral to 27 runaway shelters and their services statewide.

☎ **National Runaway Switch Board**
1-800-621-4000, 24 hours

▲ **Macomb County Youth Interim Care Facility**
4227 Bart St., Warren, MI 48091
(313) 758-7040

▲ **Off the Streets**, 10612 E. Jefferson, Detroit, MI 48226
(313) 824-4520

▲ **The Sanctuary**, 1222 S. Washington, Royal Oak, MI 48067
(313) 547-2268, 24 hours, temporary shelter
Also available from the Sanctuary:
Heading Out: A Young Person's Guide to Living on Their Own
by Laura Castleman and The Sanctuary, (1987, $2.50 plus shipping)

▲ **Youth Living Centers – Counterpoint**, 715 Inkster Rd., Inkster, MI 48141
(313) 563-5005

✎ *Runaway Teenagers* by Frances Koestler
Available from
Public Affairs Pamphlets, 381 Park Ave. South, New York, NY 10016-8884
($1.00)

✎ *Understanding Runaways:* A Parent's Guide to Adolescents Who Leave
Home and other helpful booklets are available from
Minerva Press, 6653 Andersonville Rd., Waterford, MI 48095
(75¢ plus 50¢ postage)

❏ *Helping Your Teenager Deal with Stress* by Bettie S. Young
(St. Martin's Press, 1987, $7.95)

✔ Also see resources under "Adolescence" in *Parenting and Family Life*
section.

Q When do I start to talk to my son about sex? He is 5. With so much talk about AIDS and other sexually transmitted diseases, I hope I can be calm in my discussions about sex. It's almost like one should fear sex.

A Whether you realize it or not, you are your child's primary sex educator. From the day of birth, everything that you do or say will have an impact on your child's sexual attitudes, values and behavior. The way you respond to everything that is male or female, the parental relationship, and how you answer questions directly related to sex issues will all contribute to your son or daughter's understanding and morals.

If you are open and "askable," your child will begin asking questions about sex, such as differences in sex organs and the origin of babies, even before the age of 5. These questions should be answered as directly and spontaneously as you would answer a question about the weather.

As the child matures, the questions will become more complex. Let the child be the guide to the level and extent of interest, and then share your knowledge and understanding accordingly. The child, who feels comfortable that the answers will be spontaneous, simple, direct and without reprimand or lecture, will continue to seek information and guidance from the parent.

There are many opportunities for parents to show how they think and feel about morals and values by reacting to sexuality on television or in life. Discussing these issues openly with your child will help him or her develop a healthy attitude about sexuality. Just stay "askable."

Helene Mills

A Perhaps the best method of conveying a safe and acceptable sexual lifestyle is by one's own example. Kids tend to mimic adults they admire. You can begin talking to your children about sex when you are adequately informed and therefore capable of giving correct advice and information. You should both initiate discussions and answer questions in a clear and concise manner.

My earliest recollection of discussions about human sexuality was while assisting my mother or father in preparing fish or chicken for dinner. We discussed what eggs are, where they come from and their purpose.

Anything that threatens our existence is obviously dangerous. Yes, sex may initiate disease processes that kill, and therefore sex is dangerous and must be respected. It's our choice to become parents. When we do, we accept the responsibility to properly rear and inform our children. A properly informed child is less likely to have an injurious or disastrous sexual encounter.

Charles C. Vincent

Resources

▲ **Planned Parenthood Centers** provide counseling, educational and medical services. Brochures include: "How to Talk With Your Child About Sexuality," "I know I'm Growing Taller," "I Know My Body Is Changing" and "How to Talk to Your Teenager About the Facts of Life." Addresses of Michigan affiliates are:

- 3100 Professional Drive, P.O. Box 3673, **Ann Arbor**, MI 48106
- 785 Pipestone, P.O. Box 1123, **Benton Harbor**, MI 49022
- 553 Woodward, #1337, **Detroit**, MI 48226
- 310 East 3rd St., **Flint**, MI 48502
- 425 Cherry St., SE, **Grand Rapids**, MI 49503
- P.O. Box 1069, **Kalamazoo** 49005
- 1400 E. Michigan Ave., Suite 202, **Lansing**, MI 48912
- 228 W. Washington, Suite 1, **Marquette**, MI 49855
- 820 Arlington, **Petoskey**, MI 49770

■ **"How to Talk to Your Child about Sex"** (Free)
National PTA, 700 Rush St., Chicago, IL 60611-2571
(312) 787-0977

■ *Okay, Ask Away!* A Guide to Help You Become an Askable Parent When
It Comes to Sexuality and Related Issues (Free)
Family Services of Boston, 34 1/2 Beacon St., Boston, MA 02108

❏ *A Young Man's Guide to Sex* and *A Young Woman's Guide to Sex*
by Jay Gale (The Body Press, 1988, $7.95)

❏ *Man's Body, An Owner's Manual* and
Woman's Body, An Owner's Manual from the Diagram Group
(Bantam Books, 1978, $4.50)

❏ *Raising a Child Conservatively in a Sexually Permissive World*
by Sol Gordon (Fireside, 1986, $7.95)

❏ *Raising Sexually Healthy Children :* A Loving Guide for Parents,
Teachers and Caregivers by Lynn Leight
(Rawson Associates, 1988, $17.95)

❏ *Sexual Values: Opposing Viewpoints*
by Bruno Leone and Teresa O'Neill (Greenhaven Press, 1983, $6.95)

❏ *Straight Talk: Sexuality Education for Parents and Kids 4-7*
by Marilyn Ratner and Susan Chamlin (Penguin, 1987, $4.95)

❏ *Where Did I Come From* by Peter Mayle (Lyle Stewart, 1973, $5.95)

❏ Also see resources under "AIDS Education."

Q What is the latest information regarding the effects of smoking on the family? Both my wife and I are cigarette smokers. Is this harmful to our two children as well as to the baby we are planning to have.

A Research suggests that parents' smoking has a negative impact on the family unit in a number of different ways. Because you are planning to have a third child, you will want to know that smoking can reduce the number and movement of sperm. This can lower the chances of your wife becoming pregnant.

A second major effect is on the baby. Expectant mothers who smoke tend to have more spontaneous abortions and are twice as likely to have a low-birth weight and/or premature infant. Low-birth weight and premature infants are at a greater risk for serious illness following birth.

A third way that parents' smoking affects children and each other is through passive or sidestream smoke; this is smoke that is inhaled from others smoking. This, too, can lead to low birth weight and prematurity. Exposure to smoking can increase tenfold the risk of respiratory illnesses (e.g., asthma, frequent colds, lung disease) in children and can impair their growth and development.

The major impact of the parent who smokes is on role modeling. A parent who smokes is twice as likely to produce a child who smokes.

Virginia Hill Rice

A Cigarette smoking poses a danger to each member of your family – present and future. Consider these facts:

For Yourselves:

- About 4,000 compounds are made by burning tobacco.

- Carbon monoxide gas is produced in such large amounts that it interferes with your ability to carry oxygen to your own body, for hours after smoking a cigarette.

- Hydrocarbons from the tar (2% "regular," 1% "low tar") cause lung cancer.

- Other irritants cause emphysema, asthma and chronic infections of sinus and lungs.

- Nicotine stimulates your nervous system. Within 8 seconds you will feel a "rush," hand tremors, elevated pulse rate and elevated blood pressure (10 points higher) are common observations.

For Your Unborn Baby:

- Your blood vessels, carrying nutrients and oxygen to the baby go into spasm and lose 60% of fetal blood flow.

- All of the above compounds pass into the baby's circulation except the hydrocarbons.

- Two to 3 packs a day causes depression of the newborn at birth.

- Light smoking increases the baby's death rate by 20%. Heavy smoking by 35%.

- Growth retarding nicotine passes through breast milk. Heavy smokers also make less milk.

For Your Children:

- Infants up to 2 years of age have a 25% increase in hospitalization rate for pneumonia and bronchitis.

- Lung tests of older children show decreased functioning.

I know how hard it is to stop, but you'll feel better and your family will be healthier if you do.

John Dorsey

Resources

▲ **American Lung Association**
List of clinics available. One copy of pamphlets free: "Smoking and the Two of You," "Health Effects of Smoking on Children," "It Might Have Been a Beautiful Baby," "How Not to Love Your Kids!," "Because You Love Your Baby"
18860 W. 10 Mile, Southfield, MI 48075
☎ **Non-Smoking Assistance Hotline, (313) 559-5111,** 8:30 - 5 M-F

▲ **American Lung Association of Michigan**
403 Seymour, Lansing, MI 48933, (517) 484-4541, 8:30 - 5M-F.
One copy free: "Cigarette Smoking," "No Smoking, Kids Magazine."

❑ *Smoking for Two: Cigarettes and Pregnancy*
by Peter Fried & Harry Oxoron (Free Press, 1985, $10.95)

Q **I'm concerned about my children's safety walking to and from school. How can I teach them to be street-smart?**

A First, you need to find out what there is outside of your home that could have negative impact on your children as they go to school, play with friends and otherwise conduct their daily routines. Listen to your children, even to casual comments. A large part of their education may come from their friends.

Then share the information you have gathered in an open and frank manner. Teach children specific ways to handle themselves in the variety of situations they might encounter.

Teach your children to avoid specific places where trouble seems to breed. Children should not go to secluded spots, go with strangers or accept any offers from strangers. They should avoid other youngsters known to be troublemakers or those known to carry weapons even if they think these kids are "cool."

Walk your child to school until you and he or she feel comfortable. Organize your neighborhood to keep a watch on all children and to walk in groups to school. Work in your school to monitor the halls to keep the school safe for all children.

Y. Gladys Barsamian

✔ We are so horrified by the thought of a stranger harming our children that when such an incident occurs, it becomes highly publicized, giving the false impression that there are "dangerous strangers" lurking everywhere. In reality, statistics show that crimes of abuse and kidnapping are most often committed by someone close to the child – a relative or family friend. The following guidelines, furnished by the National PTA, will help you teach your children how to keep *themselves* safe when you're not there. And remember, your example is their best teacher – practice what you preach!

How to Be a Safe Walker

Teach your children these street rules. Practice safety habits when you walk with your children to reinforce what you tell them.

O **Walk on the sidewalk.** When there is no sidewalk, walk facing traffic so you can see the cars before they reach you.

O **Stop at the curb before crossing** the street. Look left, right and left again.

O **Cross at the corner,** never in the middle of the street. Don't dart out.

O **Avoid walking into traffic** from between parked cars.

O **Wear bright clothing** in the daytime. Wear clothes with retro-reflective tape at night.

O **Walk with a buddy** or group whenever possible. Avoid alleys and deserted areas, especially when walking alone.

O **Remember that cars are bigger than you are.** Even if you *should* have the right-of-way, wait for an approaching car to stop or slow down before you step into the street.

Gangs? Not My Kid!

Children join gangs and commit vandalism or violent acts due to a need to belong to someone or something. Children join gangs at age 14, sometimes younger. Gang membership, especially among "hard-core" members, is strongly tied to drug use, sexual activity, violence and crime. It's a difficult cycle to break.

Parents *can* protect their children from a gang's influence:

O **Spend time alone with each of your children** to help convince them that they are an important part of the family.

O **Supervise your children's activities.** Make sure a reliable adult is present at all functions.

O **Help your children get involved** in athletics or other groups activities that interest them so they can feel they belong.

O **Talk with your children about values.** Let them know why you think gangs are dangerous.

O **Teach your children what to do if gang members approach them.** The best response is to WALK AWAY. Warn children not to respond with the same gesture – the gang members may be "false flagging," using the sign of a rival gang. The result could be violence.

The National PTA - 1988 Child Safety and Protection Month Kit

Street Smart Children Know

○ **Their phone number and address.**

○ **How to reach you at work.**

○ **Who to call in an emergency** (at least two neighbors or relatives, the police and the fire department).

○ **Which are the "safe houses"** on your block and in your neighborhood.

○ **Where they are going,** who they are going with, when they will be back – and that they always tell you.

○ **The safest routes to school,** friends' houses and other regular destinations.

○ **That they should never accept anything from a stranger:** candy or other food, toys, games, pets, money or gifts.

○ **That they should never let themselves be drawn into the car** of anyone except those with whom you've given them permission to ride.

○ **That if anyone threatens them, they are to back away immediately** and leave as fast as possible; also, that it's OK to scream if they are frightened.

You can make the learning of safety rules into a game. Ask your children such questions as "What if you stay late at Joey's house and it's dark when you start to come home?" At first you may not get the best answer. Discuss all the alternatives you can think of and select the best one together.

After you've played "What If" for awhile, your children may give you the answers that they think you want to hear. Now is the time for a new game that can make safety a little more realistic. Ask questions like, "But REALLY, what if you thought I'd be furious at you for being late?" Honest answers may be different from pat answers. You need to learn what children would *really* do and help them learn what's the best solution for them.

When the game gets boring and interest wanes, stop for the day. The best learning is fun.

From the National PTA-88, Back to School Special Redbook Supplement

---

Resources

■ **Block Homes Nuts and Bolts**
A guide from the National PTA provides information for setting up a "Block Home" program in your community. (Single copy free with SASE.)
National PTA Health and Safety Center
700 N. Rush St., Chicago, IL 60611
(312) 787-0977

✎ **Gangs in Schools:** Breaking Up Is Hard to Do
Booklet featuring gang prevention strategies. ($3.00)
National School Safety Center, 16830 Ventura Blvd., Suite 200
Encino, CA 91436
(818) 377-6200

■ **Too Smart for Strangers** video by Buena Vista Home Video ($29.95)
Uses humans dressed up as Wnnie the Pooh characters to gently teach children (ages 3-7) how to deal with potentially threatening situations. Available in retail outlets or through :
Buena Vista Home Video; 1-800-255-5550, ext. 480

❑ **Keeping Your Kids Safe** by Jean Brown (Monarch PR, 1985, $6.95)

❑ **Your Children Should Know:** Teaching Your Children the Strategies That Will Keep Them Safe From Assault and Crime
by Flora Colar and Tamar Hosansky (Pub. Group, 1986, $4.95)

❑ **How To Raise a Street-Smart Child:** The Complete Parents' Guide To Safety on the Street and at Home
by Grace Hechinger
(Fawcett, 1985, $3.95)

❑ **Never Say Yes To a Stranger:** What Your Child Must Know To Stay Safe
by Susan Neuman (Putnam Pub. Group, 1985, $6.95)

❑ **Come Tell Right Away** by Lynn Stanford (Ed-U-Press, 1983, $2.95)

❑ **Children Without Childhood** by Marie Winn (Pantheon, 1983, $13.45)

Q Somewhere I read about raising a "suicide-free kid."
What does that mean? How prevalent is suicide in
youngsters today? Do I need to worry about my 14-year-old?

A Suicide among adolescents is so prevalent that it qualifies as
one of the leading causes of death for that age group. Many teens
know at least one person who has attempted or completed a
suicide. Since our children are influenced by many forces
other than their parents, it is impossible to guarantee that one
can raise a "suicide-free kid." There are some things you can
do, however, to tip the odds in your favor:

Help your children develop a healthy self concept by acknowledging their strengths and refraining from putting them
down. Allow them the independence to become competent
in caring for and making decisions for themselves.

Foster a sense of open communication in your home. Let your
children know that it is safe to talk things over with you and
be themselves with you. Be sure they understand that asking
for help is a strength, not a weakness.

**Allow your children to develop a sense of control and responsibility
for their own lives** by letting them handle the consequences of
their decisions. When they are unhappy, help them figure
out what solutions they can generate rather than trying to
"fix" things for them.

**Help your children understand the difference between feelings and
behavior.** Many people have thoughts of suicide when they
are feeling depressed or hopeless. Children do not always
understand that thoughts and feelings change, however, and
that one may choose not to act on a particular feeling. One
may choose to act on a feeling in a number of ways: asking
for help, for instance, or doing something with a friend, etc.
Provide examples through your behavior and by talking
about this important idea to your teen.

Carol Mitchell

A In today's world, suicide is something parents need to be aware of and concerned about. The suicide rate among 15- to 24-year-olds has tripled in the past 30 years. More than 1,000 young people attempt suicide every 24 hours. A 1984 study by the Menninger Foundation concluded that almost 11 percent of all Americans aged 15 to 24 have attempted suicide at least once and that an estimated 500,000 new attempts are made each year.

According to William Steele, former Clinical Director of the Emergency Telephone Services/Suicide Prevention Center of Detroit and a national expert on youth suicide, the problem is far more severe than even these shocking statistics indicate because many teenage suicides are reported as accidents.

Young people themselves have described a wide variety of factors that contribute to suicidal feelings. The leading causes appear to be lack of self-esteem, feelings of loneliness and isolation, and pressure to succeed.

It's important to understand that the years from 15 to 24 are almost universally difficult ones. We as parents can make a positive difference by treating both our children and all others with respect and courtesy. One of the best ways to teach youngsters the coping skills they need is for us to set good examples of appropriate problem-solving behavior. We need to be available as a sounding board, letting our children know the value we place on them unconditionally, and provide appropriate structure and discipline without undue pressure to achieve. **We must try to be our children's finest ally.**

Resources are widely available for those suffering from depression, anxiety or overtly suicidal thoughts and feelings. All a troubled individual has to do is to get to the phone, call the operator and ask to be connected with a suicide prevention center. They exist in nearly every county in Michigan.

Debbie Stabenow

Resources

▲ **Suicide Prevention Centers** are located in nearly every county.
Check your phone directory under Emergency Numbers or Hotlines.

☎ Macomb County Crisis Center: **(313) 573-2200,** 24 hours

☎ Oakland County: Common Ground **(313) 645-9676,** 24 hours

☎ Wayne County Crisis Center: **(313) 224-7000,** 24 hours

■ *Adolescent Suicide: Identification and Intervention* ($2.95)
Community Intervention, Inc., 529 S. Seventh St., Suite 570
Minneapolis, MN 55415
1-800-328-0417 8:00-4:30 M-F

❑ *Everything to Live For* by Susan White-Bowden
(Pocket Books, 1987, $3.95)

❑ *Helping Your Teenager Deal with Stress* by Bettie B. Youngs
(St. Martins Press, 1986, $8.95)

❑ *Is Your Child Depressed?* by Joel Herskowitz
(Pharos Books, 1988, $14.95)

❑ *Suicide: The Danger Signs* ($3.95)
Your Child Has Died ($4.95)
Questions and Answers ($3.25)
Kidsrights, 3700 Progress Blvd.
P.O. Box 851, Mt. Dora, FL 32757

❑ *Teach Your Child Decision Making* by John Clabby and Maurice Elias
(Doubleday, 1986, $8.95)

❑ *Too Young To Die* by Francine Klagsbrun
(Simon & Schuster, 1984, $3.50)

❑ *The Urge to Die* by Peter Giovacchini (Penguin, 1983, $6.95)

✔ Also see resources under "Mental Illness" and "Self-Esteem" in *Parenting and Family Life*

Q My daughter is 13. I've read that many young teens are sexually active. What can I do to help her avoid pregnancy? What can I say when I talk about sex and pregnancy? What can I read about this subject?

A Open discussions and factual information are vital in preparing your child for sexual maturity. Adolescence is a time of physical maturation, hormonal changes and establishing an identity. Pregnancy results from lack of information about body development and birth control. Most adolescent pregnancy is accidental. It is a very fertile time in their lives. Actions taken during this time can create lifelong obligations and emotional trauma. Teens must understand that decisions must be taken seriously.

Having a baby can fulfill a variety of emotional needs. But adolescence is often a confused period. Teens mistakenly feel that becoming a mother might solve their problems and make them respected as adults. They see having a baby as a solution to loneliness or depression. They finally will have someone to love who will love them back – unlike other disappointing relationships. Their thinking is distorted and inaccurate.

Becoming pregnant during adolescence compounds an already difficult stage of development. Adolescent parents are less likely than other students to complete high school or to obtain steady jobs. Keeping their baby increases the chances of poverty. The inability to cope with demands of parenting result in increased child abuse, substance abuse and depression. Lack of acceptance, social isolation and rejection can result in lowered self-esteem.

Adolescent pregnancy often becomes a family crisis as parents have to assist in making difficult decisions about abortion, giving up the baby for adoption or caring for it. The psychological pain of having an abortion is often very difficult and long lasting.

Your daughter needs to understand that emotional intimacy is much more than sexual involvement. We must help her understand the many positive roles and types of activities open to her. A full and responsible life must be your ultimate goal for your daughter.

Noelle Clark

|A| Many teens are sexually active. In the U.S. it is estimated that 40 percent of all 14-year-olds will experience at least one pregnancy by age 19. The *Journal of Pediatrics* recently reported that the age of first intercourse in one study of young men was 12.

Last year more than one million teenagers became pregnant, with over half of these pregnancies being terminated by abortion along with its physical and psychological traumas. Of those who elected to proceed and deliver a child, 50 percent will not complete high school. These youngsters join a socioeconomic class that few are capable of escaping.

It is important that parents talk with their sons and daughters about sex and pregnancy with an emphasis on the physiological purpose of sex (procreation, not recreation). It should be stressed that no sex is best during adolescence. Parents and children need to plan together to promote an interest in other activities.

Charles C. Vincent

Resources

▲ **County Health Department** - Check your local telephone directory under county offices for Health Department services such as a **VD clinic or family planning counseling.**

■ **Planned Parenthood League** has offices throughout the state, offering comprehensive services, counseling and information. (See "Sex Education" for a complete listing.)

☎ **National VD/STD Hotline,** 1-800-227-8922

▲ **Sex Information and Education Council of the U.S. (SIECUS)**
80 Fifth Ave., New York, NY 10011

❏ *How to Help Your Teenager Postpone Sexual Involvement*
by Marion Howard (Continuum, 1988, $14.95)

❏ *Risking the Future:* Adolescent Sexuality, Pregnancy and Childbearing
by Cheryl D. Hayes (National Academy Press, 1987, $21.95)

❏ *Teenage Survival Book:* The Complete Revised Updated Version of You
by Sol Gordon (Times Books, 1981, $12.95)

✔ Also see resources under "Sex Education."

Q I am on maternity leave, but must return to my job to help support my family. For the baby's sake, when would be the best time for me to go back to work?

A Babies are ready for substitute care at about four months. In the first four months, the mother learns about the baby and herself. When the baby smiles she knows the smile is for her, she understands when he is fussy and ready to play or needs to sleep. The mother and the baby become attached to each other. This attachment is tremendously important in helping the baby feel secure throughout his early and later stages of development. It is his cushion for learning and growing in the future. If someone else helps the baby through the first four month to smile, to vocalize, to play games, the new parent will not feel the same sense of attachment.

During the fourth month, the baby has a " burst of learning" about himself and his world. He becomes acutely aware of new sights and sounds and grows increasingly independent. This is the time to think about returning to work, remembering the longer you can stay home, the more you will feel the baby is yours and the more intimacy you'll share.

Other good times to go back to work might be when your baby is 9 or 10 months old, or after stranger anxiety has passed and after self-feeding, sitting and crawling are achieved. Or at 18 months or 2 years, after walking, negativism or heightened fear of separation of the 12- to 16-month period are being managed. Each baby develops at his own pace, so cues must come from the baby.

When you return to work, your baby is likely to regress – go back for a little while – in his development, but if he has been given early confidence, this regression will be temporary and you'll know that you both will adjust to the separation.

T. Barry Brazelton

Q I must work to help support our family. But there is always so much to do; our lives are hectic. My husband doesn't help much at home, but he is a good father to our kids. How can we acheive a calmer, more stable family life?

A "Having it all" for working parents requires having 1.) a supportive family, 2.) a supportive work place, and 3.) quality, reliable child care. Here are ways to develop a supportive family:

Try keeping a time log for a few days. Review the log with your husband and plan for more efficient use of both of your time. Group and consolidate activities, develop routines. Make short lists of tasks to be accomplished – it feels great to cross them off when they are done.

Tame the telephone. Let it work for you to save time, rather than waste time.

Set priorities. Don't try to be superwoman. Learn to say "no."

Plan your time in advance..Allow for fun and relaxation together as a family – it's more important than dusting.

Let your children help and share responsibilities. Being a family is everyone's job.

Marlynn Levin

A Parenting is rarely a 50-50 split. Most often one parent is carrying the bulk of the load. To share the parenting role with your partner, set agreed-upon guidelines, review them periodically and do not hesitate to make necessary adjustments. It's important to clarify expectations. Each parent is responsible for communicating his or her thoughts and feelings. Some agreement on roles must be reached.

Working parents often feel guilty about time spent away from children and the conflicting energy demands of job and family. When parents are flexible and working as a team, problem situations become challenges to be resolved. Remember, communication is the lifeline of a family.

John Abbey

A **Parenting is a full-time job** – add it to full-time working and life is bound to be hectic. Working parents need to:

Spend time listening and talking to children every day.

Explain to children that when you're tired and upset from work, it's not their fault. Don't take out your frustrations on them.

Be aware that children manipulate parents who feel guilty. Give consistent discipline and watch overindulgent caring.

Above all, give children lots of love and instill in them a respect for self and others.

Debbie Stabenow

Resources

❏ *About Time: A Woman's Guide to Time Management* by Alec MacKenzie and Kay Waldo (McGraw-Hill, 1981, $5.95)

❏ *Hard Choices: How Women Decide About Career and Motherhood* by K. Gerson (University of California Press, 1985, $9.95)

❏ *The Superwoman Syndrome* by Marjorie Shaevitz (Warner, 1985, $3.95)

❏ *Super Working Mom's Handbook* by Roseann Hirsch (Warner Books, 1986, $8.95)

❏ *The Working Parent's Dilemma: How to Balance the Responsibilities of Children and Careers* by Earl Grollman and Gerri Sweder (Beacon Press, 1986, $15.95)

❏ *The Working Woman Book or How to Be Everything to Everyone* by Barbara and Jim Dale (Andrews, McMeel and Parker, 1985, $6.95)

❏ *Staying Home Instead: How to Quit the Working Mom Rat Race and Survive Financially* by Christine Davidson (Lexington Books, 1986, $12.95)

❏ *When Your Child Needs You* by Eleanor Weisberger (Adler & Adler, 1987, $7.95)

❏ *Working and Caring* by T. Barry Brazelton (Addison-Wesley, 1985, $16.95)

For additional copies of the *Parents' Answer Book,* contact your local PTA unit for special discount rates.

Books may also be ordered directly from the Michigan PTA for $7.95. (A $2.50 shipping and handling charge is applied to each order of up to 24 books.)

Organizations other than the PTA are welcome to sell this book as a fund raiser.

Michigan PTA
1011 North Washington Avenue
Lansing, MI 48906
(515) 485-4345
Group sales are available

The first "Parent Talk Page" appeared in the *Detroit Free Press* in February, 1987. It has since received commendations and praise from both parents and professionals.

- In November of 1988, the "Parent Talk Page" was honored with the prestigious **Distinguished Service to Families Award** from the National Council on Family Relations, "recognizing exceptional volunteer and professional efforts and outstanding leadership in the cause of better family living."

The page and staff have also received:

- **House Concurrent Resolution No. 849** from the Michigan State Legislature
- **A Michigan Psychiatric Society Commendation**
- **Michigan Council on Family Relations Distinguished Service Award**
- Honors from the **Michigan Children's Trust Fund.**

"For many American children, these are difficult times. Some are the victims of physical or emotional abuse; many are under-nourished; too many live in poverty in single-parent families; others are homeless; and most recently we learn of children who are ill-cared for in substandard day-care facilities. Drug abuse and AIDS threaten the well-being of a whole generation of our youth.

"Every measure which ensures the health and emotional welfare of America's young strengthens all of us and promises hope for the future. The Michigan Psychiatric Society believes that the *Michigan Parents' Answer Book* contributes to those ends."

Beth Ann Brooks, M.D.
Lafayette Clinic
President, Michigan Psychiatric Society

"Raising children presents challenges to parents at all stages of a child's life. Parents are constantly looking for support and suggestions regarding child rearing. This book is an answer to that search, providing insights from a number of experts, offering practical understanding and solutions to child-rearing dilemmas. The Michigan PTA deserves thanks and recognition for making this information available."

Eli Saltz, Ph.D.
Director, The Merrill-Palmer Institute
Wayne State University

PEPSI. THE CHOICE OF A NEW GENERATION

*This book has been made possible, in part,
through a grant from
The Pepsi-Cola Company*